Praise

"Arias will break your heart, blow your mind, make ~
the edge of everything that matters. *Momentary Illumination of Objects In*
is a phenomenal and dazzling debut that gives voice to people who live on the
edges and in-between worlds. I will carry this book near my body like a firewall
against the wrong world, like a fierce love song that will not be silenced."

~ Lidia Yuknavitch, author of *The Book of Joan*

"Inspired, challenging, heartbreaking, and uplifting—the stories of *Momentary
Illumination of Objects In Motion* are an after-midnight bar story, a foxhole
prayer, a graveyard shift confession. Arias confronts masculinity and identity
and memory and authority—as urgently needed as anything in fiction today."

~ Matthew Robinson, author of *The Horse Latitudes*

"Arias made me feel that I was being read aloud to at a bar, as if someone
was leaning in close, three rounds deep, and confessing to me their visions
of limping mermaids, and half-Dominican, half-Harlem, half-something-
else fathers, and girls counting the bullets put in their father backwards. It's
a book that makes you feel whispered to and pulled in close. It's a book that
makes you wince your eyes and re-see things you thought you knew."

~ Rita Bullwinkel, author of *Belly Up*

"*Momentary Illumination of Objects In Motion* sends us hurtling into the joys and
terrors of growing up and becoming a man. In several stories, Arias looks at
life through the unflappably calm eyes of an EMT assessing the carnage at a
fatal accident. Alert to both the fragility of humans and their resilience, Arias
finds flashes of humor in the wreckage, as well as rare moments of beauty
when humans transcend their limitations to become their best selves."

~ Stevan Allred, author of *The Alehouse at the End of the World*

"Arias illuminates the rough beauty of ordinary life with brevity and
concision. At once, both funny and stark, the stories in *Momentary Illumination
of Objects In Motion* are ferociously honest about the hard truths of our
existence, and yet still burn with love and appreciation for all the parts of our
humanity. A kickass debut."   ~ Margaret Malone, author of *People Like You*

"No floral verbosity here; Arias gets right down to the meat and bone of his
stories. Yet—or perhaps because of that style—he also homes in on powerful
imagery, revelatory metaphor, and vibrant characters who are fascinating to
watch evolve from one story to the next. *Momentary Illumination of Objects In
Motion* is a debut that pulls no punches, and Arias is a writer to watch."

~ Samuel Snoek-Brown, author of *There Is No Other Way to Worship Them*

MOMENTARY ILLUMINATION
OF OBJECTS IN MOTION

JASON ARIAS

BLACK
BOMB
BOOKS
blackbombbooks.com

Black Bomb Books LLC
Asheville, NC
Printed in the United States of America

ISBN: 978-0-9980116-5-3

First Edition
Book and cover design by Maggie Powell Designs
www.maggiepowelldesigns.com
Cover and author photo by Julie Arias

For permission requests, contact:
blackbombbooks@gmail.com
BlackBombBooks.com

For all my people

Versions of these stories have been previously published in the following:

❖ "The Great Expectations Artists" (*Nailed*, online)

❖ "Truth" retitled "Inner Workings" (*Perceptions Magazine, 2015*)

❖ "M.B. and Me" (*Perceptions Magazine, 2015*)

❖ "Writing Code" (*Perceptions Magazine, 2014*)

❖ "Landscaping Keepsakes and the Eternal Under-Bed" (*AFTER(life): Poems and Stories of the Dead, Purple Passion Press*)

❖ "The Road to Thebes" (*Nailed*, online)

❖ "Inventorying the Future's Armory"(*Blue Skirt Productions,* online)

❖ "The Golden Hour" (*Oregon Humanities Magazine, Fall/Winter 2016*)

❖ "All the Same Ocean" (*Oregon Humanities Magazine, Fall/Winter 2015*)

❖ "The Third Bullet" (*Oregon Humanities Magazine, Fall/Winter 2017*)

❖ "The Process" (*The Stray Branch, Fall/Winter 2015*)

❖ "Closer" (*Broken Pencil Magazine Fall 2018*)

❖ "Real-Life Story Problem" (*Lighthouse, Issue 15 Spring 2017*)

Table of Contents

Deer Don't Scream, Do They?   1

The Great Expectations Artists   7

Writing Code   11

Five Girls I Knew in Grand Junction as a Boy   21

M.B. and Me   27

The Golden Hour   32

Early Man   38

Landscaping Keepsakes and the Eternal Under-Bed   49

Real-Life Story Problem   52

Finding Timo *(Six Party Games for Late Night Postmortem)*   56

The Uncomfortable Augmentations of Earl Sneed Sinclair   66

The Third Bullet   71

Inner Workings   77

The Road to Thebes   87

The Case for Viable Life in Atlantis   92

Inventorying the Future's Armory   100

Closer   105

All the Same Ocean   112

The Process   118

Acknowledgments   120

About the Author   121

Deer Don't Scream,
Do They?

Two ambulance medics, one cop, and I are standing above the dying deer. There's another cop in the passenger seat of the parked patrol car. It's cold enough to wear beanies, but only the cops are wearing them. They're black—the beanies not the cops.

The deer is on her side, in the gravel at the shoulder of the road. The ambulance is parked in one lane with a busted headlight. The patrol car is parked in the opposite lane. Orange cones spread from behind the two vehicles and taper out toward the shoulders of the road, as if continuing off into the woods. Red and blue emergency lights spin endlessly on the tops of the ambulance and cop car. I can see my breath, and our collective cloud of breath, and the short puffs of breath from the grounded deer.

I'm the rider on the ambulance, the not-even-new-guy yet, the still-in-community-college-guy doing a ride-along to complete my EMT Basic requirements. If I pass my class test, and the state test, I'll be qualified to drive a wheelchair van while taking classes to become a paramedic. That's one plan.

"It just came out of nowhere," John-the-older-medic tells the cop, "and I tagged it. Or...it tagged us." He points back to the broken left headlight of the ambulance. There's a crimped patch of brown fur stuck in the side of the grill.

"Gotcha," the cop says nodding with his eyes closed. He keeps his eyes closed.

"Must have broken two of its legs, at least," says Seth-the-younger-medic, with more energy than his older counterpart. "Initially it went down, but then it got back up. Its legs were all

1

wobbled out, and when its body hit the ground the momentum carried it halfway into the gravel and…"

Seth keeps moving his hands and feet and mouth, keeps over-explaining until the cop says, "Gotcha," and opens his eyes again.

Seth stops talking and, eventually, stops moving his hands.

John shrugs his shoulders.

Seth had called the deer an "it," but "it" looks like a "she." And "she" looks like Bambi's Mom to me.

And Bambi's Mom is on the ground kicking at the loose rocks with her hooves like she's trying to start an antique motorcycle from a horizontal position after having to lay it down. Her fur is mostly brown with scattered isles of spotted white. The blood speckles at the sides of her mouth and snout make the fur tinged pink in places, dark red in others. The air smells like old pennies.

"Must be pooling most of the blood inside her," John-the-older-medic says. He turns to me and says, "You'll see that in people, too."

Bambi's Mom keeps looking up, wide-eyed, from her broken position. Her eyes are the deep brown of comfortable blankets. Big, soft, brown eyes. Those eyes are probably the reason I've given her a gender, the reason I'm sure I'd be a shitty hunter. They're probably the reason some people refuse to eat meat. Not me, but some people. Even scared, those eyes make this deer look incredibly kind.

"Yeah, my cousin hit one coming back from Bend," the cop says. "BAM!" he says while clapping his hands together. "Fucked up his Ford like nobody's business," he says. "It was a big mother, though. And that son-of-a-bitch just kept running. Probably died in the woods somewhere, you know?" He shakes his head. "Damn shame to see a deer like that, though. Takes all the sportsmanship out of it."

The wind pushes through the branches of the trees around us. It's been dark all day with cloud cover, and it's just getting darker.

The passenger door of the cop cruiser opens, and the second cop gets out. He shivers for a minute (just a little shiver, like working out the kinks), shuts the door, and walks over to where we stand.

"What should we do now?" the second cop says. His face is more flushed than his older partner's. He looks like he probably doesn't have to shave but does anyway.

"Well, *Brian*, we do our job," the first cop says. "We put it out of its misery."

Brian looks at his partner, then at the medics, and then at me. And by this point we all know that Brian must be the rookie. I think that Brian-the-rookie-cop looks like me, not in his features, but in the way he stands on one foot and then the other, the way he keeps fidgeting around. He looks from the deer to the stopped traffic in both directions. His eyes are like the deer's. Soft and wet and big and brown all over.

Cars keep lining up on either side of those orange cones that John and Seth put out after we hit Bambi's Mom. It's getting to that in-between point where the light seems like it might stay an angry red bruise in the sky but then decides to peace out.

I look at Brian. He looks back at me. For a second, I feel like we can both tell that neither of us has ever killed anything besides fish and insects and probably more than a few conversations. It's something in our eyes. I can feel the shame souring between us, our unspoken truths emasculating one another. We look away at the same time, and I don't look back. I train my eyes on the ground, where the deer lies, willing myself to watch her fur sporadically rise and fall. I watch her hooves kick in wild spurts and lie still and her body go nowhere. I'm trying to grow a callous over my vision thick enough not to care, because I don't want to be weak here.

I wonder if Brian is thinking the way I am about how the deer at our feet won't be able to play anymore reindeer games. And if that makes him as sad as it makes me. I wonder if the deer's offspring are watching us from the forest, plotting their revenge; if they'll grow up all dysfunctional from seeing their mom die in front of them and become drug addicts or something. Does she even have kids? Do those kids have names? Do they have other woodland friends? I wonder why my mind's plugging in Disney storylines when confronted with the reality of a dying deer. I wonder if maybe this medic thing isn't the profession for me after all. How the hell am I supposed to stick people with needles, and defibrillate hearts back to life, and bandage broken bones and shit, if I can't even watch a deer get hit and die on the side of a road without getting all sad about it?

Bambi's Mom keeps kicking. Keeps licking the pink of her snout with her too long tongue. I feel like she keeps arching her neck up to look at me. Straight at me. She looks stunned, but not stunned. Like if she could form words she'd say, "Wow, I didn't see that shit coming," and still be sweet and kind and witty about it but nonetheless broken; like she'd ask for a last cigarette and then cough and cackle and smile.

"Brian!" the older cop says to his partner. "Deer's in pain."

"Right," Brian says. "Yeah," he says. "Okay," he says, and draws his gun from its holster a little too fast.

The older cop, the medics, and I all take a collective step back. The older cop's hand pats the air in front of him slowly like he's either telling Brian or his gun to, *Take it easy.*

Somebody in one of the stopped cars starts honking in short and long blares, like they'd been born with a steering wheel for a face, but are nevertheless trying like hell to communicate. Some car in the opposite direction honks back like they're happy to finally find somebody that speaks their language.

Brian-the-rookie-cop spreads his feet apart and clutches his gun with both of his hands in front of him. His arms fully extended. Elbows locked out. Brian's bent slightly forward at the waist like it's the only hinge in his body. His nose flared-out and his lips disappear into his face. He sucks cold air in and exhales steam. Brian keeps edging toward Bambi's Mom in this stiff-legged position, approaching her from the backside, to avoid getting kicked by her hooves. His black boots baby-step across the gravel— never really leaving the ground, just sliding, leaving ski marks— and his face blanches slightly below his black beanie. The closer he gets to the doe's head, the more I notice his arms shaking. By the time he stops, his arms are in full tremble. I don't want to know what his face is doing. I focus on the deer's irregular breathing, the steam clouding over the panic in her eyes, the stopped traffic lengthening.

A man steps out of a stopped Dodge and starts walking our direction. His driver's door is left open.

Brian takes a little in-breath through the side of his mouth.

And,

BAM!

His gun goes off like a door being kicked in. I jump back. The medics jump in place. The older cop grumbles. The noise echoes out into the trees to either side of us, and funnels out over the roofs of the parked cars. The man, who seconds ago had gotten out of his Dodge, runs back to the open door, and dives in, and lies belly-down across the front seat with his boots sticking out of the driver's side.

Bambi's Mom opens her mouth and starts screaming like a human baby on fire, like some kind of horribly played brass instrument in a death-metal basement-band. Her hooves kick wildly at the gravel. Pebbles bounce off our clothing. Seth-the-rookie-medic backs up while holding his arms crooked over his face.

"Jesus Christ, Brian!" the older cop yells. "You shot it in the fucking neck?"

"Sheeeit," John-the-older-medic says through the side of his mouth.

Seth-the-younger-medic backs up farther.

There's a small hole in the doe's fur at the side of her throat. I'd expected a peeled back banana of flesh. A gaping wound. The hole seems smaller than it should be.

Brian panics—with the deer shrieking and gravel flying and dusk coming—and shoots his gun at her again.

I wait for something on the doe to explode but nothing does. Instead a second hole appears in Bambi's Mom's neck. It's pretty close to the first hole. It's just as small. Bambi's Mom bucks and kicks harder, like she's trying to run sideways into the afterlife and failing. Flailing.

"Fucking Christ," the older cop says. He puts the muzzle of his gun close to the doe's temple. Fires a bullet into her skull.

The doe stops screaming.

Her legs stop pedaling.

Her neck and head slump and roll out across the gravel like a clump of thick, brown carpet.

The wind stops blowing.

Seth stops retreating.

5

Nobody's honking.

John-the-older-medic runs a finger across his moustache slowly.

The doe's eyes stop bulging, but keep staring.

I look up from the doe and accidentally catch Brian's eyes. I've been avoiding them. We're still just two guys that have never killed anything except fish and insects. But now we've seen something die together. And Brian looks sad about that, like he wishes he'd taken more care to shoot the doe right the first time. Or even the second. Or maybe he wishes he hadn't shot it at all. Or never gotten out of bed this morning. Or chose a different profession.

His partner looks up from the ground. He steps to Brian's side and puts a hand on his shoulder.

The older cop grunts before saying, "Good job, son," out of the corner of his mouth into Brian's ear. And Brian nods. But you can tell that neither one of them believes Brian did a good job.

The older cop walks back to the patrol car, shaking his head. He opens the door. I watch him put the CB to his mouth.

John-the-older-medic turns to Brian-the-younger-cop and says, "You guys good with us getting out of here?"

Brian holsters his gun but doesn't say anything. Instead, he turns and walks to the patrol car.

The older cop walks over and nods and says, "You guys can go."

We pick up our orange cones. They fit inside each other perfectly, like a nesting doll set. John stores them in a side compartment.

As John and Seth and I climb back into the ambulance, I hear the radio crackle up front.

John answers the crackle with our location.

More crackle.

"Yeah, the rig's still drivable," John says. "Copy that. Put us on it." He clicks the toggle switch for the sirens.

Seth turns back to make eye contact in the square cross-through that visually connects the cab to the back of the ambulance. I'm sitting in what they call the "airway seat," twisting to look at him.

"All right, kid," Seth smiles, "you ready to see some real shit?"

The Great Expectations Artists

A halfie, a midget, and an Italian walk into a music store. It sounds like the beginning of a bad joke. A horrible riddle. They each have at least two other names. The halfie goes by Jason and Oreo. The midget goes by Sean and Stubs. The Italian goes by Tony and WOP.

I'm the halfie; half Dominican, half whatever.

There's no political correctness between us. It's entirely pre-PC here. None of us has a desktop at home. The Internet doesn't exist. We're just three kids exploiting the ugliest parts of our heritage to destroy any future expectations anybody might have for us. We have infinite identities, and insolent disregard, and an insatiable hunger for Bay Area music. Digital Underground. Too $hort. Hieroglyphics. Tupac.

Oakland-based music keeps our Portland heads bobbing.

We each enter the music store in the Fred Meyer, in the heart of Rockwood, at different times. We are not friends here. We're just three separate music concierges who, together, make a joke with no resolve; a riddle with no purpose. We're more like an illusion. More like a mirage.

I go in first and head to the Jazz section in the far left corner, nod to the thirty-something clerk as I walk by, hold my pants up at the crotch so they don't slide right off my ass.

Sean's next, entering a couple minutes later. He goes straight to the Rap section at the middle of the store. He's flipping through tapes behind the plastic T tab with his small, chubby fingers. Those fingers are part of the reason we call him Stubs. They're part of the reason he's always trying to prove himself to us. Those fingers and his tiny stature are also the reason that the thirty-something

7

clerk immediately looks away when Sean catches him staring. The clerk looks away and doesn't look back. I'm not really needed as a distraction, but I'm here to give the clerk a justifiable alternative.

I'm still in the Jazz section *justifying*: looking back constantly, turning the tapes over and over in my hands, readjusting my pants. I'm fingering "Bitches Brew" like I even understand Miles Davis yet, like I ever fully will. It's a backwards flirtation dance between me and the clerk: eye contact with quick-cuts to the right and left, ambiguous lip contortions, incessant crotch grabs. Him in pleated khakis. Me in ironed jeans. Both of us at work, in different ways.

Just before the thirty-something clerk goes for the phone, Tony enters in a pair of Levi pants that actually fit, a Gap tag self-sewn to the back pocket as an upgrade.

Tony says, "I just need a player with the right balance of bass boost, sir." He points to a Walkman on the half-wall behind the register. "What about that one?"

I don't even need to look to know that this is the moment that Too $hort and Tupac start disappearing up Sean's cuffed sleeves and into the sides of his coat lining. He's not just a thief, he's a magician. He's an artist. With the hours of practice he's put in, he's a master. His clothes are riddled with invisible pockets and hidden slits. Anything the size of a pack of cigarettes, or a cassette tape, is Bermuda Triangled into his smoothness.

By the time the clerk turns around to hand the packaged Walkman to Tony, Sean's disappeared what was in his vicinity, onto his person. He shakes his head, starts walking. Just like that. Smooth.

But behind the clerk's head I see security walking toward the music store entrance—just one overweight guy in one of those puffy, black, cop jackets. Maybe they got cameras in here between the last time and now. Maybe the thirty-something clerk just pushed a button somewhere. Maybe this is why magicians don't perform the same trick too many times in the same city, because eventually the audience sees the strings.

Sean and the security guy meet at the entrance/exit. One coming. One going. Security's looking down at Sean. Sean's looking back up at him. He's definitely not the same security that picked Sean completely up off the ground by his collar last week at the Tower Records store. That time Sean had yelled, "You're not my daddy! You're not my daddy!" and the guy had dropped him (looking all stunned and self-conscious) and Sean got away because Sean knows how to think quick. But maybe this security knows that security somehow. Maybe they play cards together or something. Maybe Sean's fucked.

I think I see Sean panic for just a second. It's just a little shiver, just a tiny tic at the crease of his right eye that you really have to watch to catch. Then Sean's face breaks and he bares the most innocent, freckled smile; his sandy hair poking out the sides of his Dodger's ball cap.

Security opens his mouth and says something that I can't hear. He nods all friendly. He looks like he wants to pat the top of Sean's head. Tell him to stay in school. Tell him to keep drinking milk. Instead, the security guard turns and nods at the thirty-something clerk. Thirty-something turns and nods toward me.

Sean walks out of the music area, past the grocery registers, past the line of carts before the sliding doors. When I can't see the back of Sean's parka anymore I start nodding to myself.

I hear Tony say, "I don't think that's going to be enough bass, man," to the clerk.

Security walks to the Jazz section, looks me up and down, and says, "You got a problem with your pants, son?"

A halfie, a midget, and a WOP enter a music store and come out a mulatto, a little person, and an Italian. They come out a blasphemy, a half-pint, and a Guido. They come out a probably, a maybe, and an unknown. They come out with so many cuffed doves and flying card tricks that people start believing what they're showing them. They take turns putting themselves in boxes, then cutting the boxes in half, then cutting the halves again. They keep cutting 'til there's nothing left on the stage but sawdust and hand tools.

And the audience is invited up to sift through the remains, claiming, "Here's proof of this and this and this." But there's never proof. There's only deception and flair and misdirection. There's only the dust of expectation and fluttering feathers around them.

And then the wind picks up.
And, poof!
Just like that, Tupac's playing on the tape deck.

Writing Code

Part 1: More Romantic Gaming Music (His Story)

When you're a kid with no street cred, more orthodontic hardware than a silverware drawer, and logging three-hundred-plus hours a month online on Fairies and Monsters, you take what you can get. You find the glitches in the system. You find the clauses in every contract you've made within every ill-lived past life, and you exploit them. This is how you override the karma luggage and bad luck you've accumulated. You use your brains and your internet-earned bronze to bust your way into the reality you wish you had.

When you dream, it's always in color.

Look, at precisely 0715 every school day, Leona Harold exits the front door of her residence and walks with perfection down her driveway. Picture a runway model with actual hips. Now make those hips wiggle. Picture her wearing those red-rimmed glasses to read from her science book in fifth period. Picture yourself fantasizing about a classroom invasion just so you'd have a chance to rise from your seat, with devout shoulders, and protect your princess from some muscle-bound, mentally crippled thugs. I know. I know. Picture yourself actually mouthing what you'd say to Leona when she finally recognizes what you mean to her. And turns to face you. And says, "Thank you!"

And you say, "It's my pleasure, Leona." And then whisper, "It's my pleasure," even more debonair.

Picture that dumbass Dick Danson throwing a wadded up sheet of unfinished homework at you. Imagine that projectile bouncing off your gaping mouth and landing at Leona's feet. But you don't have to imagine too hard because it actually happens.

This is reality: the rest of the class laughing and pointing at you from their designated seats. Leona looks from that wad of homework on the floor and straight into your eyes. Her lips curve upward, and for a single moment she isn't laughing at you, but smiling with you; her eyes glistening under the fluorescent lighting.

If you're paying enough attention to those clauses in your contract, and you've been duped like me into a less than desirable real life and want out, then you've probably already considered the holiday glitch.

See, people think that holidays have to do with religion, or patriotism, or consumerism, or some such shit. But they're wrong. Holidays are wormholes for people like us. They've primed the public to overlook abnormal behavior, or at least forgive it. If you look at the binary long enough, you stop seeing the zeros and ones and only see the spaces in between them. You start looking for the code behind the screenshot in everything. You realize that every great wizard of the past was just a nerd, like you, with a bigger hard drive. The God you signed that bunk contract with is the biggest nerd, writing the divinest code.

When Halloween rolls around, you use the power of anonymity and don your best disguise to gain access to the parties you were never invited to. Maybe you drink too much trying to plot your next big move, and they find out you're not really Iron Man, but by then it doesn't even matter. You've already distorted reality. You've already jail-broke your life, Tony Stark style.

For St. Patty's Day, you log onto *theluckyclover.com* until you get the wish you wanted to pop up on the screen in the first place; the one that says: "That special someone will notice you today!" Then you don your emerald green **KISS ME I'M IRISH** t-shirt and make a strategic walking route through the school halls between every one of your classes, based on maximizing your face-to-faces with Leona. You walk with your chest held proud. Hope that one of your passes peaks Leona's interest enough to make her consider that you might actually have a pot of gold hidden in your pants.

"Well, I'm no leprechaun, but..." you picture yourself saying while pushing out your chest and sucking in your gut.

For Flag Day, you rise to full staff. For Memorial Day, you ask Leona if she remembers when the two of you were in Mrs. Duncan's second grade class.

She doesn't.

"We were in class together, back then?" she asks.

She used to smile at you back then. All the time.

For Valentine's Day, you make a grand gesture that never sees the light. On Valentine's night, you cry, just a little. Don't act like you haven't been there. You have. We have.

For Christmas, you usually hibernate. You don't sleep because you can't, with that much Code Red Mountain Dew surging through your system, but you also don't leave the house. You usually stare at your computer screen until your eyes bleed. Not this Christmas, though. Well, maybe on Christmas day—maybe even some of the days leading up to it—but before Christmas break you have a mission. We have a mission. And it all starts with Leona Harold leaving her house at 0715 every school day morning.

"Ronnie, do you want some cocoa?"

"Not now, Mom, I'm busy. Don't open the door."

"Your father and I are downstairs. Always."

"I know."

If you're like me, you'll get up early every day leading up to that break and plot the course. You've done the math. You know there are eleven and a half blocks between Leona's front door and the school. She walks these alone. This is the playing field. Her house and the school grounds are hazard zones. They are the regions where your advances will be shot down, hands down. You're not stupid. You can outthink life. You need to make your move within a neutralized area.

So you work with what you've got. You maximize it. There are 264 feet in a city block. That gives you 3,036 linear feet of total traveling distance, just over half a mile. That's 36,432 inches of opportunity. Even if you only get your hands on fifty mistletoe to hang from fifty different branches and telephone wires along that route to school, the odds of creating a glitch in our favor are enormous compared to the off-holiday season. The odds are a hell of a lot better than winning the lottery.

13

"Ronnie, there's a package for you."

"Thanks, Mom. Just leave it outside my door."

The thing is, there are hundreds of lotteries. Any idiot over eighteen can win one of those. We know this. We know we only have one shot at Leona Harold. We've got to be smart. We've got to keep playing and storing our mana in cyberspace and the real world. We've got to keep looking for the loopholes. Nobody's going to help us. We have to have faith in the glitches. We have to keep writing our own code; keep watching for the same purple cat twice. This is going to work for us; we've done the math.

This is it.

Are you ready?

Don't puss out on me.

The sidewalk's frosty, but not icy, while we wait. There's still a layer of snow everywhere. This is good. It's better traction than ice. It lessens the chances of us falling hard and not recovering.

We're playing the game where we watch clouds form from our breath and count them. It soothes us. The breath clouds are rising to the rhythm of *Battle of the Wind Fish* from *The Legend of Zelda: Symphony of the Goddesses* soundtrack playing in our head when we see Leona appear in the distance.

She is walking east on 10th Street, perpendicular to our current route on Vermont. If we slightly increase our gait, we have the chance of *accidentally* rendezvousing where the two streets intersect. We speed our pace and slow our breathing. We think of more romantic gaming music. Let it play. We clench and unclench our left hand because it's just one of our many nervous tics that we've embraced. With every footfall we're stamping ones and dropping zeros in a single file line of un-fuck-with-able code.

We're so caught up in manipulating game play, and looking up for our pre-placed mistletoe, that we really do almost crash into Leona at the corner. All this planning and it's still almost a real accident. There is no one on the street besides Leona and you. Don't ask me how this happened, but this is exactly how we would have written the code if we could have. Maybe we actually are writing it. Maybe this is karma getting right with us.

"I'm so sorry," we say. "I wasn't paying attention."

It sounds believable because it's true.

"It's all right, Ronnie."

She remembers our name!

We had planned on casually looking up at this point. Of haphazardly spotting the mistletoe attached to the streetlight above our heads. But we don't.

"What are the chances?" is what we're supposed to say here. It's what the code we wrote calls for, but we don't say it. We're blowing our chances at a first kiss because we can't look away from Leona's light green eyes. We've never looked someone in the eyes for so long without flinching before. There is a sadness we've never noticed among the darker flecks of green. There is something we can almost touch there.

"Ronnie?" she says. And we pray we're not crying.

"Yes, Leona."

"We're going to be late for school," she says with a half-smile, her palms pressed to the outsides of her jeaned thighs, her shoulders slightly shrugging in her light blue wool coat.

"You're right," we say, unrehearsed. "I'll walk you the rest of the way." And we realize we sound confident.

She looks back toward her house and then down at her feet.

"Okay," she says with a shrug.

As we walk along the sidewalk, the backs of our gloved hands graze hers. We ask about her brother, who we once mistook for her uncle.

She asks, "Whatever happened to your buddy, Zach?"

After the fifteenth mistletoe we walk under, we stop counting them. For the first time in our young adult life we've stopped looking for wormholes. At some point, we stop writing subscript and just start to enjoy the screenplay surrounding us, this walk with Leona.

For me, the walk never ends.

In my game story, Leona and I never arrive at the school. When I replay it in my mind, that walk is represented by the trueness of ones and the wholeness of zeros. But it's this space between the numbers that I'll spend the rest of my life trying to recalculate: the proof of the biggest nerd, the presence of the divinest code.

Part 2: Dear Diary
(Her Story)

April 26, 2017

Dear Diary,

Today was shitty. I walked home with Debra and Susan and all they could talk about was Darren and Bradley. I thought the twin fantasy was a guy thing. I guess not, because here's Debra and Susan going on and on about how *SWEET* it is that they're dating the Hardy Boys.

Well, they don't actually call them the Hardy Boys (were the Hardy Boys even twins?). Whatever, the point is that Darren and Bradley are twins, and Debra and Susan are like best friends, and it all seems kind of incestuous, you know?

I mean, big deal if they're mirror images of each other.

"We can only tell them apart because Darren has the mole on the right, and Bradley has the mole on the left."

"Really, Susan? Big fucking deal. You guys are going to have like three-headed babies or something. Do something unique with your hair. Do something REAL." That's what I wanted to say. But I didn't.

No, I didn't really mean that. I didn't want to say that.

I don't know, maybe I did.

Diary, what the hell is happening to me?

I've known Debra and Susan since like second grade, but I haven't been able to stand them lately. And I know it's not them, not really. It's me. Not the way Frankie told Rita it wasn't her it was him, but it *actually* was her. In my case, it's actually me, and I'm not just saying that.

No, you know what? Maybe it isn't me. Maybe that's what I need to admit to myself.

Listen to this:

The other day Debra said, *"Are you SURE you're not on your period?"* just for saying I didn't feel like going to the pep rally. She sounds as stupid as Darren now. And trust me, Darren is a complete dumbass.

But, you want to hear something even stupider? Instead of going to the rally, I sat up in my room on my computer reading message boards that were talking about Ronnie.

Oh, you don't really know about Ronnie yet, do you Diary?

It's been months since I've last written in you. Sorry about that. Life gets busy, you know? The point is that Debra has been acting like a bitch and Debra + Darren is a stupid looking name for a couple, right? I'll never date someone named Larry, or Lloyd, or Lionel. Not only do I not know any hot guys named that, but L+L would look ridiculous on a park bench. Alliteration? UGH! Just find someone with a different first initial, you know? It doesn't seem that hard.

Anyway, where was I? Oh, right. I've been thinking about Ronnie because something happened. Hold on a minute.

Okay, I just had to bang on my annoying brother's wall. He's playing that melancholic music by that old guy that nobody can understand. On *vinyl*. On HIGH. I don't know how long he plans to live here, but he's like old enough to have a record player, so he's got to be old enough to have his own family or something. He's got to be old enough for me to be an aunt already. I should be an aunt by now.

Great, he just turned that crap up louder.

Okay, I need to talk about Ronnie. I just need to do it. So, here we go.

Me and Ronnie have gone to school together for a while, maybe forever. He's just one of those kids, you know, who seem nice but aren't superhot or outgoing or anything. He always wore those retro arcade game shirts. Like a lot. A ton. He's that kind of kid. That's what I know about him...knew about him. Maybe he kind of knew me? Or thought he did? I don't know. He usually turned away real fast when I'd catch him staring. So, you know.

Then around Christmas I caught him kind of lurking around my street. Maybe *lurking* is a bad way to describe Ronnie. He wasn't scary or anything, just more interested in me than I was in him. He was really quiet. I just didn't really know him. I know that now. I figured he was weird and shy and liked tape measures a lot (we'll get to that later) and, I don't know.

I know you don't know this, Diary, because you're not real, but what I'm getting at is that nobody's seen Ronnie for months. And it's my fault. At least, partially my fault.

After Ronnie disappeared, the news started showing his parents pleading for his return. And his mom was like really pretty, but really teary, so it made her less pretty, but there was still something there, you know? And Ronnie's dad just looked like a dad. And when the reporters started interviewing them, I don't think they knew if they should have been pleading to some kidnappers or to Ronnie or what. But I knew. They should have been pleading with me, just days before he went missing, to not have been such a bitch.

The worst thing was when the police started saying they were looking for Ronnie *"in regards to detailed, hand-drawn layouts of the inside of the school"* and *"strange markings on the street routes leading to the facility"* and other stuff they found inside the desk in his bedroom. Who the hell calls school a "facility" anyway? Ronnie didn't. I'll tell you who: Cops. Cops are dumb.

But guess what? They said my house was on Ronnie's map. And that my house was designated with a heart. That's kind of sweet, right? I mean, of Ronnie to do that.

They said that kids like Ronnie, who are on the internet all the time, can't decipher reality from fantasy. Yeah, like Debra and Susan can? The news said they found digital receipts of *"a large amount of mistletoe, which the suspect had purchased online."* They said that much mistletoe could have been used to poison the Winter Solstice punch.

They thought Ronnie was going to go all passive-aggressive Columbine or something.

Didn't they see all the mistletoe hung from the poles on my route to school?

Ronnie was a nerd. He wasn't a killer. He's a loner, not a lunatic. Maybe he was a bit of an overly persistent charmer, but he was a good person. He is a good person.

JUST LOOK UP! I wish I could tell the cops that and have them hear me. I don't know why people don't just look up anymore. Well, I kind of get it. I guess it took me a while, too. But when I finally did, I'd never seen so much mistletoe before.

That was from Ronnie. For me. I think.

Doesn't that make you like him a little more?

I know this sounds stupid, because I know people look at me all the time (I'm not trying to be conceited, it's just true), but nobody's ever looked at me the way Ronnie did the last day anyone saw him. And if all that mistletoe could have been for me, then Jesus, I can't help but be flattered. Debra and Susan would never go through that much work for me. Okay, that's a different thing, but you know what I mean. No guy I know would climb all those poles just hoping for a non-tongue kiss from Yours Truly. How goddamn sweet is that?

That whole time I thought Ronnie was lurking around he was actually doing so much more. And during that walk, he talked to me like normal. I mean, I get it, I can see his plan now. All that mistletoe he hung, and he didn't even try to kiss me.

All those blocks we walked—and it was nice. But right before we get on school grounds, Susan walks up and says, "Why are you walking with *him*?"

And guess what I said, Diary?

I said, "Who, *him*?"

I said, "Oh, he's just stalking me."

Can you believe that? Knowing what you now know that makes me sound like the biggest bitch ever. I mean technically maybe he was stalking, a little. But even when I said it, I didn't really mean it. I was mostly kind of joking. I was joking. I was only being the Leona I was supposed to be. God, I wish I hadn't said that. I wish he hadn't heard it. I wish Debra hadn't started laughing and that Ronnie wouldn't have thrown his backpack down and run across the field and into the woods. And never come back out.

Those woods just stay woods all the way to the river.

I'm not insinuating anything, Diary. I don't think Ronnie's dead. I don't care what they say, I know he's not. And part of that's probably because I can't let myself think it, but part of it's because I don't feel like it's true. And let's face it, if anything, this whole scenario has only shown us that Ronnie is too smart to die in the woods or in a river or something so stupid.

L+R

That doesn't look so bad, does it?

19

I still don't know what I'm doing, Diary. I know you can tell. Do you think I'll get better? I spend more time on message boards online now and down by the river, just walking. I carved L+R in a tree in the forest a little bit ago with a nail file. It's harder than I thought it'd be. I totally ruined that file.

Every week after they stopped searching for Ronnie, in those woods, I've smuggled blankets and food from my house and left them by the same tree. The same tree I carved our initials. There's probably a ton of squirrels with diabetes and huge nests out there. But I'm just trying to make my wrong, right. And on the plus side, mom says she's never had more room in the linen closet before.

A part of me wishes that I would have told Susan that there's something about Ronnie that takes a minute to see. And I wish that Ronnie could have heard that, and understood what I meant by it. Because once you see it, you can't un-see it. I'm still seeing it. Right now.

A part of me wishes I would have yanked on Debra's hair until she started screaming. The way she laughed at Ronnie running. The way she said, "Look at him run like that." Another part of me wishes I would have run after Ronnie that day. And even another part of me wishes he never would have noticed me at all, so this would have never happened. But if I'm being most honest, that's the smallest part of me.

You know, I can't stop thinking that our last walk should have never ended. I can't keep looking at myself in the mirror the way he did before he ran into the woods: like I'm the biggest letdown in the world.

I'm trying to be a better person. I'm trying to live a semi-normal life. I really am.

I'm putting you back now, Diary. I don't know for how long. But we'll talk again. I promise.

–Leona

P.S. I just got back in from the woods, after going to the tree that I carved L+R in, and somebody's carved a heart around it. I know. That's hopeful, right? That has to mean it's him.

Jesus, I've got to go. Dad's yelling about where all his camping gear went to.

Five Girls I Knew
in Grand Junction as a Boy

Ann

At age six, by the irrigation ditch behind the yellow house. We're digging holes and catching crawdads by their tails. Ann picks one up by its midsection and talks to it. She talks through it.

Her thin lips say, "Let me pinch you," while dancing the crawdad back and forth in front of me.

Ann has the biggest smile ever. And there's always a smudge of jelly, or a stain of Kool-Aid, or a streak of dirt at the corner of her mouth. We bury her metal M.A.S.H. lunchbox, full of keepsakes, behind her house as a makeshift time capsule. There is a baseball card in there, a book of matches, a strand of each of our hair. Her blondeness is doing magic tricks, disappearing and reappearing in the sunlight.

Ann and I watch *Rambo* and *Texas Chainsaw Massacre* while her father drinks Hamm's and crunches the cans in his hand and air-balls them into the kitchen. I keep thinking about that poor blonde woman at the Leatherface Family dinner table trying not to die. The way her head keeps bobbing over the metal bucket, so close to being sawed off, and Ann kind of peeking through the cracks between her fingers and making faces through them at the TV. The way she flinches at every crunching of a Hamm's can.

I don't know what became of Ann. But I picture her smiling the way she did in the only picture of us I still have—the crook of our kid arms wrapped around the back of each other's necks, backlit by the dining room window in the yellow house—my half-fro silhouette juxtaposing her feathered, white-magic wisps.

Maria

At age eight, Maria was pint sized. We were the same age. Her brother was older than us, but we were also friends. Maria was the one who handed me the bread and the glass of milk after I ate a habanero pepper at her family's breakfast table. The rest of her family sat around the table laughing so hard that eventually I had to start laughing along with them. And when I gave in to that heat behind my eyes, there were the back slaps and the "*Aye, aye, aye, Hason*"s from her father and the comradery of it all.

Maria had jet black hair; her skin was the darkest Guatemalan. She was a mini stick of dynamite thrown at the heart of a small backwards town.

And, once, Maria and I played her version of "house" where we both squeezed into Midnight's doghouse in my front yard, and Maria laid flat on top of me and put her lips to each corner of my mouth and said, "This is what grownups do, right?"

And I was too scared to move, so I just laid there. And she just laid there. And I tried to understand how grownups ever wanted to do anything else.

Natalie

Natalie was in my class from kindergarten through second grade. She was the kind of kid whose beauty was overlooked by the cruelty of other kids.

Natalie laughed and smiled without making a sound. She saw everything. She wore sweaters (that were too big) over ill-fitting, long-sleeved button-ups. She got picked on by our classmates for seeming meek. But when she painted, during art time, she used her forearms and palms and elbows in body throws and finger jabs. She'd end up with paint on her cheeks and clothes, and the sides of her desk, and the tips of her reddish-brown hair. Her eyes remained focused. Her full lips curled upward, and her hair stood out like she was touching one of those big crystal balls with lightning in it.

She liked to draw circles. She put dots in the middles of them.

Natalie might have been the first real artist I ever saw in action, before I knew what the terms "artist" or "action" *really* meant. But I could only admire Natalie from afar, because I knew that lightning could either kill you or give you special powers, and you wouldn't know which one until you were hit by it. And I was pretty sure I would die.

I picture Natalie as pure energy, striking where least expected. In my head, she's going back to the main drag of Grand Junction to draw circles on the houses of the boys who used to call her a witch. And she's spray painting dots on their lawns and laughing. And smiling. And laughing. And saying, "What? What's so funny?" still completely unaware of her powers. Or maybe just too humble. But she's always covered in acrylics. And always conjuring the beyond.

Lupe

Lupe: who lived at the other end of our complex, when we had drug dealers for neighbors. Lupe: of the white loose-necked sweaters, black stretchy-pants, and white high-heeled boots with the cuffed tops. This is Lupe at age nine. Lupe: trying to kiss me after dark on the sidewalk behind the apartments in the rain.

Me: afraid to be devoured like multi-colored gumdrops. Afraid that I would stick in her teeth and not know how to get out. Me: worried about weird shit, always. Me: wondering if it was possible to get sucked into an alternate dimension (like that garage band in the Saturday morning cartoon I watched). Me: wearing my favorite pair of corduroy pants, every day, just in case it happened (getting sucked into that other dimension); and wanting to be stylin' there.

Lupe: trying to kiss Phillip by the culvert in a red jacket. Lupe: kissing Robert by the jungle gym in jean shorts. Lupe: who I worried about, even then, because she was so full of love and so willing to misplace it. And I wondered if we were both sucked into that other dimension (Lupe and me), if we could escape our fates by playing music on cartoon keyboards and over-sized bass drums like that garage band in the opening credits before they became animations. Me: wondering if it was possible for people to save each other like that.

Amanda

Amanda is way older than me. She's one of the camp counselors at the day-camp my sister and I go to called Moon Farm. It's the summer between first and second grade. At Moon Farm, we ride horses whenever we want, and dig up fossilized shells, and trade the shells in for candy at the General Store. Amanda's hair is dirty-blonde worn straight. She's here to help watch all of us, to make sure a horse doesn't fall on us. When the summer ends, she'll be going to college to do something in the arts. She talks about "the arts" like they're a form of magic.

On the last day of camp, Amanda is sitting on the carpet in the day area with me and a dozen other kids, watching Disney's *Robin Hood*.

Three-quarters of the way through the movie, Amanda bends close to my ear and whisper, "That's it."

And I whisper back, "What's it?"

Amanda says, "We dress you up like a girl, the way Robin Hood and Little John did when they tried to save Maid Marian. Then we enter you in the talent contest."

I say, "But it didn't work out for them." I say, "Lil John's melons fall out while they're trying to get away."

Amanda says, "But it's the right thing to do. Are you brave?"

Maybe, I think. "Yes," I say.

So when the movie ends, Amanda and I go to the costume room. And she finds a red and black can-can onesie that looks like a swimsuit with ruffles at the hips. I don't have hips. Amanda finds a garter belt and a pink flamingo headdress. And I go into the bathroom and put on everything she hands me.

When I come out, Amanda nods at me and says, "Perfect!" She picks up a black, feather, wraparound boa and says, "When you go out there, just keep kicking. And don't forget to smile."

Before the music starts, I'm standing in the middle of the stage with an ocean of kids and camp counselors sitting on the floor of the auditorium in front of me. My legs feel too long being exposed all the way up. The boy before me wore a cape and did card tricks. He was okay. I'm trying to convince myself that this is being brave. I'm trying to remember to smile. In my head, I keep hearing Amanda saying, *We can win this!*

The speakers behind me crackle and erupt in '20s era flapper music. I nod my head for a minute to get the rhythm right. A woman's tinny voice starts singing. I start kicking high in front of me, alternating legs to the tempo of the snare drum and cymbals. My knobby knees flail. Amanda is all big-eyed at the side of the stage, bending her knees, snapping her fingers and bobbing her head. I keep looking at her for confirmation that I'm doing it right. I kick higher every time she gives me a thumbs-up, or a double-thumbs-up, or a pumping air fist. I'm kicking my feet chest high, chin high, over my head while simultaneously looking out at the audience and keeping Amanda in my periphery.

I hear some kid in the front row say, "I don't know that girl."

I kick higher. I try not to sweat through the nylons I'm wearing. Some other kid says, "Hey, that's a boy."

Amanda and me, we're in this together, so I keep kicking, but my movements are less fluid, less peppy, less crisp. Amanda's still snapping and bobbing. She's shaking her shoulders and hips just off-stage. She's trying to show me new moves to incorporate on the fly. She's kicking in front, and then behind her, while maintaining jazz-hands. But I don't think I have the kind of balance it takes to pull off those moves in oversized high heels.

I hear another kid up front say, "That's a boy in a leotard." He starts laughing.

A camp counselor says, "Billy, I'm sure he's not a retard!"

A second counselor says, "You can't know that for sure, man."

And suddenly I realize what I must look like up here. My skinny legs cross-dressed. My cheeks flushed. The makeup Amanda applied streaking down my face with the sweat.

I stop kicking as high.

I'm not Robin Hood. Robin Hood wouldn't do this just for a grand prize of a Pizza Hut coupon. I keep kicking until the music stops and the sea of kids and counselors just stare up at me. There are a couple of awkward claps, mostly from counselors that are always trying to get everybody *psyched*. I exit the stage, trying not to trip.

Amanda stands with her arms completely spread, waiting for me. I want to hate her for putting me out there like this. But when I reach her, she's still smiling at me. She's not smiling because she thinks it's funny, she's smiling because she thinks it's awesome. She thinks *I'm* awesome. She wraps her arms around me and plants kisses all over my face. She says, "My hero!" and nuzzles her chin into the top of my head. She says, "Who gives a shit what they think?"

I still don't want to let Amanda down. So I don't tell her that I do. I give a shit. Instead, I nod into her chest. I act brave. I say, "Yeah, what do they know?"

M.B. and Me

Anytime M.B. and me would start running into people whom we used to know, but hadn't seen in a while, we figured there was a greater-than-normal chance we'd be dead soon.

So when we ran into Tabitha (from fifth grade), and Jimmy (from Rockwood), and Indian Johnny (who should have still been serving time in McLaren, but wasn't), we knew that these weren't just coincidences. These were the kinds of hints Death dropped if you were paying attention. Each triplet of run-ins with old friends and acquaintances was just Death giving us a heads-up; a little time to mentally prepare for her. See, you can't really override fear, but you can acclimate to the inevitable.

At fourteen, we'd sip box wine from tall plastic cups on M.B.'s parents' back porch. His mom would be stamping out Kools in the ashtray and spinning the stories of the Four Horsemen, and the Seven Bowls of Revelations, and how Earth would be one bloody-as-hell mess right before the end. She'd talk about the Rapture like it was more than just God kidnapping people. She'd talk about locusts with faces of men and teeth of lions and tails of snakes.

But all that shit was way scarier than the way *I* pictured Death. I envisioned Death as a redhead in tight pants and all the right curves. She was bad ass and worked in threes. Everything sacred works in threes. Threes and sevens. The Bible loves those numbers.

M.B. and me would run into Stubs (the greatest little thief I ever met), and Brenda (the snitch), and Montezuma (the Sureno who was supposed to only be fourteen but looked like a goddamn man already), and we just knew we wouldn't make it through the week.

But seven days would go by and we'd still be alive—all the cortisol built up and souring our systems.

It didn't matter if we ended upside down in cars on the Butte, or stumbling blacked-out into traffic, or running from packs of dudes who jumped from the backs of trucks with baseball bats and brass knuckles and 2×4s. Shit, one night five Asian dudes ran at us, out of the Plaid Pantry on Glisan, spinning belts over their heads as if winding up some ultimate spanking machines. But no matter what happened, we always woke up the next day. Some scrapes, some bruises, some welts, but still alive.

M.B. and me started wondering if we could die.

We double-dipped into hallucinogens and let it ride. We started telling everybody, everywhere, to "Fuck off" as a method to our pseudo-scientific mortality testing. We drank so much malt liquor that pieces of our minds are still just blank spots floating somewhere. We made the world our laboratory.

That redhead, Death, was nowhere to be found. There were no horsemen to be seen, let alone four horsemen, let alone an army of two-hundred-million horsemen with heads of lions and tails of snakes. And the only bowls we ever saw were the ones in the kitchen sink that needed to be washed before using them for Honey Grahams. Plus, the San Andreas Fault still hadn't broken loose in Cali, let alone that big-ass earthquake that was supposed to have swallowed up a third of the planet.

I wanted to tell M.B.'s mom that Revelations really wasn't making much progress.

Instead I said, "I really thought we'd be dead by now." And I told her why.

And in her half-pidgin speech she said, "Whaaaat? You boys aren't gonna die, yet. And when you do, ain't nobody gonna leave you a note in your lunch sack about it."

"What about Revelations?" I said.

"Oh, that's different," she said. "That's bigger than you two."

M.B. and me ran into the landlord, from the apartments my family used to rent on 162nd, and she just shook her head and walked the other direction.

On the Fremont eastbound, we saw this girl I used to date, and she locked eyes with me for a second, then turned away from me in her bus seat and stared out the window.

On the MAX train, I saw the counselor that once told my mom I was "too bent on self-destruction," and he was holding his baby, or at least *a* baby—it could have been somebody else's.

And this once-ominous triplet was now just another boring-ass reminder that Death was probably still coming but being really, really slow about it. Like her car broke-down on the I-5 months ago, and she was like, "Fuck it, those guys can live for a while."

One day, we ran into Donnie (the Skinhead) on his ten-speed, and he was all hopped up on some shit and pissed off. Donnie pulled a handgun from his waistband and leveled it at M.B. Then at me.

He said, "All right, half-breed. Which side's the nigger half?"

I didn't say anything. I didn't tell him that the half he was talking about was actually Dominican. And after what felt like an hour (but was probably less than a minute), Donnie stuffed the gun back in his pants and pedaled away.

And I wasn't even that angry or scared. I was just tired. I felt it everywhere in my body. I looked at M.B. and saw that he was tired. We weren't even seventeen yet, and we were already old men.

M.B. and I stayed tired. We wandered the streets less. We got day jobs.

We had kids with girls who grew into women.

I married my woman.

I stopped believing in the end of everything. And then found better things to believe in.

Seventeen years later, my mom's having lunch with me, my wife, and my now teenage sons. After swallowing a bite of her roasted veggie sandwich she says, "Did you know that Silvia Brown doesn't see any humans left on Earth in the twenty-second century?"

She really likes Sylvia Brown.

Mom's always been into prophets. She's the one that first turned me on to Edgar Casey and Nostradamus back in the day.

But I figure that by now, she knows, like I know, that nobody knows shit.

I say, "How can somebody even prepare for something like that? I mean..." I glance at my sons to make sure they're not internalizing any of this doomsday stuff.

Mom smiles and says, "Haven't you and M.B been preparing for the end of the world since you were teenagers?"

It catches me off guard. I almost choke on my sandwich. Laughter erupts from me before I can stop it. Mom starts laughing because I'm laughing. My sons kind of look at me sideways, and kind of laugh, but mostly wonder. My wife just shakes her head at the table.

Later, I pick up M.B. at the apartments he manages. We're sitting in my car in the parking lot. The plan is to go see the original *Let the Right One In* at Cinema 21 downtown. I tell M.B. what mom said about us, and he laughs until he coughs and his knees bounce off the glove box in front of him.

He says, "Holy shit, that's funny, man!"

Then he says he saw Shari two days ago outside of Rite-Aid.

He says, "Yeah, she had a stroller with her, and the place where the baby should have been was filled with empty cans."

I say, "Yeah, I saw Ronnie and his mom at Papa's Pizza the other day. They didn't look so great. I remember them having more teeth."

I say, "Julie and I saw Travis tweak-dancing down the sidewalk between 172nd and the library, and I kinda wanted to stop to see if he needed anything but didn't."

M.B. and I both get quiet for a minute. Whether I like to admit it or not, I'm still superstitious. A piece of me still feels like that angst-ridden kid I used to be, only with more adult fears and less stamina and more debt.

A knuckle-knock on the driver's side window breaks our silence.

I turn the key to the accessory position and there's the dinging sound. I push the button that rolls the glass down, and it grumbles and squeaks, like the rubber guides are trying to keep it up, trying to tell me to just start the car and drive away, trying to force me to stop looking at every little thing like it means something.

I see the red locks first, spiraling out the front of her black hoodie. She's backlit by the only working lamppost in the parking lot. My pupils dilate, trying to see better through the darkness and the rain. The wind's blowing in. I feel that long-ago certainty that this is our redhead. And Death, she smells hot. Like J. Lo perfume and gunpowder and clenched jaws and flashbacks.

They say your life passes before your eyes just seconds before you die, but I don't know about that. I think it takes days, or months, or years. I think that shit takes a lifetime. But in this moment, in this parking lot, I just wish I didn't have to leave my wife and kids and mom and sis, and M.B. and his family, and the kid with the giant zits I haven't seen for twenty years but still think about, and Ronnie and his missing teeth, and Papa's Pizza and its taco pizza and breadsticks, and the feeling of rain blowing in through my open driver's side window.

Even that, man. I'll even miss the wind, and the fucking cloudy days, and the uncertainty.

Death's still staring down at me. She puts her left hand on her cocked hip and eases back. She's all attitude stiffening, and neck stretching, and shoulders rolling and straightening like a giant locust with the teeth of a lion and tails of a snake.

And my throat is a sticky dry cobweb. My hands are creepy clammy.

I say, "What the fuck? Really? Now you want me?"

Death just laughs. She licks her lips.

She says, "Who you getting fresh with, motherfucker?"

She says, "Look, you gonna move your hooptie up out of my spot, or does my man have to come down here and move it for you?"

The Golden Hour

I'm riding shotgun in the ambulance, navigating us to a vehicle-versus-pedestrian call we've just been tapped on. I'm picturing all the possibilities in my head, all the things we'll have to do when we get there.

There'll be a quick triage to find out how many in total are injured (pedestrians, driver, plus or minus passengers). Police and Fire will establish a blockade, using their vehicles and orange cones, to prevent other vehicles from driving into the scene and clipping one of us. We'll have reflective vests on, and we'll still have to watch our six. There'll be backboards and neck collars to apply. We'll park our ambulance at a defensive angle that allows for a quick egress to the hospital. But right now, we're still just trying to get there.

I tell my partner, Mark, to turn left on Farmington.

He says, "I got it. I know where this is, man," and toggles the siren to a warble tone while approaching the intersection.

And he does know where this is. I know he does. He's been doing this ambulance thing for years now, maybe decades. I'm the newer guy. I've seen a lot of things in my first couple of years, but there's still a lot I haven't seen. Some things you hope you never see.

Dispatch comes over the radio and says Life Flight's on standby. If this patient is in a bad way, flying to the hospital rather than going by ambulance will shave precious minutes off of the *Golden Hour*—a euphemism to describe your best chance of surviving a life-threatening injury, if you get to advanced care in time.

There's radio static inside the cab of our ambulance, and then dispatch says, "The pedestrian is possibly trapped under the vehicle."

I think of the size of an SUV compared to a person. I think of all the possible internal and external injuries that correlate with different parts of a body being trapped under something that size. A person's spleen can rupture and bleed out from being punched hard enough in the left ribcage. A severed femoral artery can cause a grown man to bleed out in less than two minutes. There are a lot of car parts that can impale a person.

When the dispatcher speaks again, there's a difference in her voice. Dispatchers are trained to remain calm. And she would probably sound calm to anybody else, but after hearing her tap hundreds of calls, I know something's off. She lilts. The lilt in her voice hits the hardest when she says, "The patient is a *pediatric male*."

In drug dosing, a pediatric is anything from infancy to adult weight. In legal matters, the range extends to eighteen years of age. In my mind, I'm praying that our patient is closer to the adult size. For just a second, I picture one of my sons under an SUV— TJ is twelve, Taber is six—and I immediately suppress the vision. Thoughts like that aren't helpful; not while getting to a call, not while treating your patient, not while going to bed at night. Not ever, really.

I look over at Mark, who's driving with complete purpose and focus. His eyes are swiveling from the side mirrors to the windshield, scanning everything on the street in front of us, looking for anything that might T-bone us from the sides. Suddenly, Mark puts the brakes on, and I jerk forward as he maneuvers around the left side of a yellow Volkswagen that's coming to a skidding stop directly in front of us.

This happens more than you might think—people just freaking out when they hear sirens. I kind of get it. But there's a reason why there's a question on your driver's test about what to do when an emergency vehicle is approaching: it's so you don't slam on your brakes and anchor it right in front of one. Mark's still so focused on his driving that he doesn't even say anything. Not "Learn to drive, Buddy!" or "Really? Really?!" with one palm up, flabbergasted. He just swerves around the Volkswagen without even blinking. I'm impressed. This is what Zen and the art of ambulance driving looks like. Mark is a master, and these streets are just concrete rivers, and we're flawlessly following the path of least resistance.

In my head I'm back to mentally forecasting the scene. I'm still wondering if it's a leg, or an arm, or a skull trapped under that SUV. Dispatch told us it's a kid. I keep hoping it's not. A lot of things change when you're working on kids. For one thing, kids' heads are proportionally bigger than adult heads. If I was Rain Man, or a mathematician or something, and I ran the numbers, there would probably be a higher chance of the kid's head being under that SUV than an adult's. I don't run the numbers. I don't know how to do that. I don't want to know how.

Another thing about kids is how long their bodies can compensate—and how abruptly that compensation can give out. An adult's vital signs usually trend downward gradually to a less life-sustaining condition, so you can chart the decline and take actions. But a kid can go from looking great to being almost dead in the blink of an eye.

I'm hoping it's not the kid's head or torso. I'm hoping that he just looks trapped.

You never really know how bad most calls are going to be until you get there. Most "car into building" calls we go on are just people who accidentally put their car into Drive instead of Reverse when leaving the convenience store, the liquor store, the dry cleaners; they're low impact with minimal injuries. Most "unresponsive patients" are actually awake and talking when you arrive. A lot of them even try to talk their way out of going to the hospital. But you can't go into any call thinking everything's going to be okay; you have to prepare for it to be bad, to be the worst.

We start to see congested traffic in front of us, so we know we're close. There are two lanes of traffic in each direction. It's a main street, not a side street. The possibility of a higher speed of impact is greater here.

A crowd of bystanders clusters on the sidewalk, many with their hands over their mouths. There's an SUV with a broken-off passenger side mirror. There's a large dent in the passenger door. The SUV is upright in the middle of the road, standing perpendicular to the flow of traffic. The vehicle is empty. There is a boy lying on the ground, face up. He is surrounded by people who are forming a half circle in the street around the boy. These people have done what cop cars and fire trucks and orange cones do; only they're protecting the patient with their bodies.

I key the radio mic and say, "Medic five-four's arrived."

Mark and I get out of the ambulance. Both of us grab our kits and together we make our way to the patient.

"Who was in the car?" Mark asks a man standing by the SUV as I kneel at the boy's head.

I see a man standing next to the vehicle raise his hand.

I hear Mark say, "Is there anybody else injured?"

I don't hear what the man says. I kneel next to the boy. He looks a little smaller than my older son. The boy looks up at me, and I tell him I'm going to hold his head still for him. I tell him to try not to move it.

I say, "What's your name?" and he tells me.

"How old are you?"

"Ten."

His eyes are big and scared and glistening with tears. He wiggles all of his fingers and toes when I ask him to. The boy says his back and stomach and legs hurt. Mark palpates the kid's belly and the boy winces. We don't find a lot of external injuries on him besides some knee abrasions, but it's what we can't see that's most concerning to us. It's the way the boy winces when Mark presses on his stomach. We need to keep an eye out for abdominal and flank bruises forming, and altered mentation, and decreasing blood pressure, and any other signs of internal bleeding.

I turn to a man with a moustache standing closest to me and ask him, "Did you see the accident?"

The man nods and says in a Spanish accent, "*Si*...Yes. This boy ran into the street for his *pelota*, for his ball, and that car tried to stop. The car, it skidded sideways, and then tipped over onto him."

"That car," I say, nodding my head toward the damaged SUV, "was on this boy?"

"*Si*," the man says.

"How is it not anymore?" I ask.

The man spreads his arms out toward the crowd around us. "We lifted it off of him," he says, raising his shoulders as if to say, *"Of course we did. What else would we do?"*

For a brief second, I think of how much bigger an SUV is than a human. I think of how much smaller a child is than an adult. I think of how much can be achieved when people are moved toward action.

"Is he going to be all right?" the man says.

"I hope so."

I look down at the kid. "You're doing great, buddy," I say. "We're going to have to get you on this hard board, but all of this is just to help you. Okay?"

He nods his head between my palms. And I wince a little because it'd be better if he held his head still.

"Try not to move your head, buddy," I say. I leave out the *"Okay?"* this time. The boy keeps looking at me, and then his eyes start getting tired.

"Hey, buddy," I say, and he opens his eyes again. I do this every time his eyes start to close. We package him onto the backboard and load him into the ambulance.

We rendezvous with Life Flight at a nearby school football field. Mark and I and two firefighters approach the helicopter from the side, ducking down, with one person on each corner of the stretcher—the wheels bumping over the grass. We load the boy into the bird with its blades spinning above us.

I hear the flight medic yell, "Hey, buddy!" to the kid and see his eyes open again. I smile at him, briefly.

Once the boy's secure, we take our empty stretcher back to the fence line. We watch the helicopter ascend in a cloud of swirling dust. The dust settles and the helicopter becomes a dot in the sky, getting smaller and smaller. It's so much quieter without the sound of the rotors.

I turn to Mark and say, "Those people put that SUV back on its tires. They pulled it up off that kid."

"Yeah," he says.

"That's fucking cool," I say.

"Yeah," he says.

"Yeah," I say.

I look at the ground for a second. I don't tell Mark I want to call home and talk to my kids. I don't tell him that those people have restored a little bit of my faith in humanity.

"Hey," I say. "You think he'll be all right?"

Mark's been doing this longer than me. He can probably predict better. He knows more, has seen more. He's all Zen in traffic mayhem and unfazed by everything.

"You know," Mark says, nodding, "he just might be." But there's a lilt somewhere in Mark's voice that I just barely catch.

Early Man

Thowa runs out the glass double doors of the Plaid Pantry, with a half rack of Coors under each arm, as the cop cruiser screeches to a stop in the parking lot in front of us. Before the cops inside the cruiser can get out, Thowa throws one of the half racks directly at them. The box of beer wheelies up the windshield and explodes on the flashing red and blue light bar. The cops scrunch down in the cruiser's seats. Cans of beer fizz in the air and hit the ground and spinout. Thowa pinches the remaining half rack of Coors between his bicep and ribcage and makes to run along the side of the cruiser.

Squeaky blasts out of the Plaid Pantry, on Thowa's heels, juggling too many 40 ouncers of St. Ides between his hands and armpits. He loses bottles outside the doors. Glass shatters on concrete. Remnants roll into the gutter. He repositions the remaining bottles and cuts along the side of the storefront.

I streak out behind Squeaky, straight toward the street on the opposite side of the cop car from Thowa, with two sixers of Budweiser. I fucking hate Budweiser, but I couldn't find the Mickey's grenades I was looking for fast enough. I couldn't think straight after hearing Old-E lay on the horn of his Chevy Caprice in three long blares. Morse code for: MOVE. YOUR. ASS. And right after those blares, the shriek of the Caprice tires peeling off on wet pavement. Old-E ghosting out.

Both doors of the cop car open at once. One cop bolts opposite me toward Squeaky. The other runs straight for Thowa and lunges. His lunge comes up short. The cop slides across the asphalt. Scrapes his chin. The sound of metal on concrete. Leather stretching somewhere. Teeth grinding. I turn back in the direction

I'm running. I've gotta get to the street. Thowa's strong enough to squish a dude's head between his hands, but he's all strength, no speed. Behind me the cop's fingers have hold of Thowa's ankle. He goes down. I hear both or their bodies crunching along the ground. They're gonna need skin grafts taken from their asses and reattached to wherever.

When I glance back I don't see Squeaky and the other cop. They must have disappeared around the corner of the store. My shoe slides for a second as I push off the concrete onto the roadway. Converse have shit for traction. I almost roll my ankle. I look back to see Thowa turn and try to punch the cop in the head.

Shit. Man, only Thowa!

I'm younger, but even I know that you can't outpunch or outgun a cop. You have to outsmart him. Outrun him. Basic. Now, it's not gonna be anything like the time Officer Krumbine made a dent in the hood of his cruiser the shape of Tony's face. Or the time they twisted Sean's arm so hard that it snapped in two. If they catch us, they're gonna kill us. Cop guns in our mouths. Our bodies lining their trunks.

My feet lick across the street as another cop cruiser bends the corner. Both of the cop cars (the one at the store and the one at the corner) are pretty much Old-E's Chevy Caprice (the one that's not here, the one he ghosted in) only slightly newer, with light-bars on top. More sirens scream in the distance.

Where the fuck are all these cops coming from?

I'm running toward a guardrail. On the other side of the guardrail is darkness. I don't know if it's a cliff or an embankment. I know I'm seeing nothing but treetops in front of me and pissed cops behind me. So. Fuck it. I leap the rail without slowing.

My body tumbles through blackberry bushes and wood mulch. I hit elbows, neck, ass, feet—repeat—on stumps and sticks and rocks and fallen leaves. Repeat. Both sixers of shit-beer go flying out of my hands into the treetops or loosen themselves and burrow under the sticker bushes. One can tumbles down the embankment with me, wedged in the crease of my crotch.

I see: sky, ground, beer-crotch. Repeat.

Sky, ground, beer-crotch.

Leg blow. Back blow. Blackness.

My eyes open to red and blue lights flashing above me. Trees changing colors like Christmas in the movies. They're beautiful. Everything feels so peaceful. I must be dead. This is why people come back from near-death experiences being like, "Shit, I ain't 'fraid to die no more." The feeling of having no feeling. Such a relief.

Then the all the feeling floods in hard. Fresh aches in my back and neck. The way my arms burn with fresh scrapes. The fear of cops. The fear of imprisonment. And I realize that I can't be dead. Not yet.

I look at my crotch. My last can of shit-beer is gone.

Some cop yells from the guardrail above with a voice sounding like how my fourth period Lit teacher, Mrs. Wilson, used to reenact the voice of Simon LeGreed from *Uncle Tom's Cabin*. "You can't run from us," the cop shrieks. "We're gonna get ya!"

I sit up in the mud and moss. My multi-colored, button-up, silk shirt is in shreds. My previously fresh-pressed and starched, white Dickie pants are soaking wet and ripped at the knees. There's dirt pushed into the pleats. There are green smears that aren't coming out, ever. The duct tape strips that kept the under-cuff of my pants hidden are a twisty mess at my ankles.

The cop above yells, "Let's get the dogs out here!"

Shit.

Flashlights scan the tree trunks and sticker bushes in front of me.

"We got your friends up here. There's no getting out!"

"Fuck. You," I say under my breath. But the *fuck* is weak and the *you* is weaker.

I listen for Squeaky but only hear mic squelches. If Thowa and the cop are still fighting in the parking lot, I can't hear them.

As much as I hate to admit it, this Harriet Preacher Stowe cop motherfucker might be right. Maybe there is no getting out of this one. I don't think I can make it through the woods in front of me with all the sticker bushes. I can't go back up the way I came without getting caught. I don't know this area well enough, yet. Mom moved us out here a couple months ago to keep me away from trouble like this.

There's trees, trees, darkness, more trees. But...wait. There's something just sticking out of the embankment, the length of two apartment buildings away. I roll onto my hands and knees. My body hurts already, in ways it shouldn't with all this adrenaline. I half crawl, half walk, half amble toward what looks like a small black hole. A giant drainpipe. A portal to somewhere else. A thorn punctures the sole of my Converse, the sole of my foot. God damn it! Skin is being pulled from my palms by every blackberry vine I use for traction. A million twigs snap under my knees, my feet. Radios squelch above me.

The cop yells, "We hear ya!"

I stumble. Fall. Stumble. My burning palm lands on something cold, smooth, metal. I hold the cold. Pull it out of the ivy beneath me. It's one of the Budweiser cans that broke loose during my fall. And it's found me. I've found it. I wedge the shit-beer in my front pocket. The can feels cold on my thigh. I keep crawling. Keep looking up at the shadows playing high on the trunks of trees.

From the outside, the inside of the drainpipe is all blackness. It's the place bodies are found in the movies. There's ankle-deep standing water. It's definitely big enough to hide in. Didn't Rambo do something like this? I can't remember how those small town cops caught him at the end. But they caught him. I know they did.

I hear the Harriet Preacher Stowe cop yell, "You got the dogs? You got the dogs, yet?"

I can't see any light on the other side of the pipe, if there *is* another side. It could just end at a grate or a wall or who knows. I feel for the shit-beer can with the palm of my hand, shake my head, and crawl into the darkness on all fours.

The inside of the pipe smells like parking lot dumpsters and bad weed and Rose Festival Honey Buckets all wrapped up and burned together. My knees scrape on every corrugated ridge. I can't tell if my shins are bleeding or just wet. I move my hands with the same knee, like some wind-up kewpie doll teetering forward. I've never moved like this in my life. But for some reason, right now, it feels safer. I'm not caught, but I'm literally in the gutter. Good and bad. The way Squeaky got street cred from so much juvy time served. Good and bad. The way that one cop told mom that Al was getting arrested if he came back to our house, and actually meant it, and another cop choked me out with gloved hands, for some stupid shit, and didn't think twice about it. But that was before. Before before. Good and bad. Good and bad. Good and...The standing water on the pipe floor is making everything heavier. My socks each weigh as much as backpacks filled with a night's worth of paint rattle cans. Rattlers. Boas. Anacondas. Are there killer snakes in the northwest? There must be. Down here, there must be. Deformities and emerging species. I'm going to grab something submerged and slithering, I just know it. Grab the tail of some insane raccoon that's gonna chew my face off.

My baggy white Dickies are sticking to my skin, dripping. My black Chuck Taylor's are fully fucked. My feet itch like a fresh head of cornrows just got braided on them. My first beer run, and I'm beer-less, homeboy-less, crawling like Tim Robbins through the forever tunnel hidden behind the sexy movie poster of a cavewoman. But I don't have money-once-embezzled to retire with after this. I just have this shit-beer can. This ruined outfit. We should have just had Old-E buy the fucking beer. I barely know him, but I know he's old enough. He's, like, twenty-seven. And we had the money. And that's the thing.

But here's the catch: You don't become a man by having older men take care of shit for you. *"You become a man by acting like one."* Thowa had said that on M.B.'s mom's porch while ashing his Newport into the black and yellow ceramic dish. M.B.'d made that dish in our fifth grade class, four years ago. My mom still has the blue and red ceramic dish I made for her, in that same class, on her nightstand. She keeps the earrings that look like owls with emerald eyes in it. But right now, it's not about those ceramic bowls or those emerald owls. It's not anything. Or, shit, maybe it is. Maybe it's about everything. All of the big and little things I won't be seeing if those cops catch me.

I can feel the cuts on my hands and knees already getting infected. I can feel sea monkeys setting up shop in my body. There's moving silt on the bottom of the pipe. I hope it's silt. I can feel bits of nature floating on top. Bits of amoeba. Bits of shit hiding in

African water that Mr. Scott shows slides of on the white screen in Science class.

There's something Thowa said. How his pops used to run up in fools' houses to toss the places. *"He'd do it quick, the way beer runs are done. Quick in. Quick out,"* he said. *"And you know why I started beer running? You really want to know?"* And I couldn't see his eyes, but they sounded not-right. And I swear I thought he was gonna say it was to go to jail and be close to his dad, or some shit. But instead he said, *"Because I knew I'd be good at it."* And we all stood there on M.B's mom's porch wondering what we could be good at. And then Thowa told us about his first run. How smooth it was. How badass it went. And Thowa's beer run stories became blueprints of badassedness. They became the wisdom of substitute fathers. The ultimate in legendary man-shit. And who doesn't want to be a legend, man?

I reach with one hand and one knee. That smell. Goddamn, what's that smell? I keep expecting a dog to run up through the drainpipe behind me, bite my hamstring, and start shaking his head back and forth all pissed off. Keep waiting to have teeth clamp onto my belt and concussion me like a ragdoll against the metal walls. What happens if a cop dog attacks you in a drain pipe? Does he just kill you and drag you out? By the neck? By the head? By the crotch? How fucking embarrassing would that be? My head hurts. My crotch itches.

I move one knee with the same hand. The other knee and hand on the backside fearing the next reach, fearing being submerged in the amoeba water too long. Fear of going forward and fear of not going forward.

I stop and listen. No dogs.

Just me and my heavy breathing.

And I can't get locked up. I can't. If I'm locked up who's gonna make sure some guy like Al doesn't wiggle into mom's life? Who's gonna watch out for my little sister with all these scamming cats out here? How am I ever gonna get a job with a beer-run record? My head's heavy. All the dirt I picked up on the fall into the woods has mixed with my Worlds of Curls hair product and is creating jacked up dreadlocks. I've been crawling forever and my eyes are just now adjusting. And the air's changing. And... I can see it. I see it. The end is coming.

There's no grate. No wall. Just more woods.

I summersault out of the blackness of the drain into the darkness of the forest and the can of Budweiser falls out of my front pocket alongside me. I look at it. Pick it up and wedge it back into my pocket. I'm back on the side of the street where the Plaid Pantry is, down an embankment at the edge of the parking lot where the shit-beer can came from. The trees are still flashing blue and red, but there are fewer sticker bushes on this side, no flashlight beams.

I hear the cop say, "Oh! The dogs are here? Great!" But his words are muffled. He's facing the wrong way.

If dogs are coming, I've gotta keep moving. But I don't hear dogs. This guy doesn't have any idea where I am. And for the first time in my life, I'm on top of these cops. For just a second, I have the upper hand, from down here. I'm doing circles around them— more like backflips, more like somersaults. And that cop's yelling in the wrong direction because he's not expecting mental gymnastics from someone like me.

And I have to see them. Just for a second. See these guys that think they know everything yelling at trees.

I crawl up the wet grass, staying low. Everything I'm wearing is beyond soaked. All of me stinks.

I lay on my belly, my body slanted down the slope. Only my eyes peek through the grass over the embankment. Cop cars face all kind of directions. I don't know how many. I look for Thowa and Squeaky, but I can't tell if there's anybody in the backs of the cruisers. The lit up Plaid Pantry sign is hovering in the sky, blanking out the stars around it.

Across the street, two cops are looking over the edge that I used to be down. They crane their necks in sync with their flashlight beams. They stand with their asses out like giant chickens.

Another cruiser pulls up beside the chicken cops. Two cops get out. There are so many cops. It's like watching ants in the ant farm on Mr. Portchick's desk in math class. All their energy put into something they think is so important, but isn't.

And then I hear them. Not the ants.

The dogs.

Barking and growling. They sound like hungry, insane motherfuckers drooling at the mouth. Trained to detect and kill the smell of poverty and teenagers and sweat and badness. And I stink like all of that.

I'm turning to bail back down the hill when I'm frozen by a sound I'm not expecting. Like tiny demons. No, not demons, children. Like children trying not to laugh. I roll back on my belly to see all three cops snickering into the cuffs of their jackets. Giggling and nodding their heads at their black boots. One cop puts a finger up to quiet the rest of them. He throws back his shoulders, juts his chin way out in front of him, and barks hard into the forest on the other side of the street.

And I get it. There are no dogs. Just un-hilarious cops. Just barking pigs.

And these guys think this is all so fucking funny. After everything. After Thowa's future skin grafts and Squeaky's imprisonment and Tony's nose and Sean's arm, this is just all a hilarious game to them.

I pull the can of Budweiser from my pocket. It's a giant red, white, and blue bullet with a liquid shit center. The cold aluminum is sleek and solid in my hand. It's the most solid thing I've ever held. It doesn't even feel cold to me. It's part of me. An extension of my arm. An extension of everything fucked about all of this. I look at each of the cops nodding heads. I get lower on the embankment. Pull back. Aim the can. I wait for the cop to start barking again.

"Arghh, Arggh, Arggh..."

The Budweiser leaves my hand. It disappears above me. It reappears, spinning, just before it crashes through the "P" in Pantry. There's an explosion of carbonated electricity from the Plaid Pantry sign. A short-lived fireworks display, hissing and fizzling out, above us. Bass. Tracers. Faders.

The cops are covering their heads with their arms, looking around like kids scared shitless. They reach for their holsters while still hunched, like one of those first pictures of man on Mr. Scott's evolutionary chart by the chalkboard, *Homo erectile*. And I want to jump up and dance and say, "Ahhh, motherfuckers, how you like me now!"

But I don't. I slither back down the embankment with mic squelches erupting behind me. I become one with the weeds and the grass and the undergrowth.

I reach the bottom of the embankment and stay at the bottom, running parallel to the street, hunched over away from all of this. I stay below grade with the radio squelches fading behind me. I don't hear the cop barking anymore. By the time I figure I must be about halfway home, I hear the real dogs barking.

I stop running.

There's a creek in front of me, and after that, everything goes level with the street. I've gotta go up.

Before I go up, I put my head close to the water and quickly try to wash out as much dirt as I can. It's impossible to get clean, with all my hair product, but it's something. I pull off my shredded silk shirt, sweated-through tank top, and once-white pants—now a Swamp Thing greenish-brown. I pull off my soaked socks. I ball everything up and stash them under some bushes. If I'm going up, I can't take this shit with me. Fucked-up clothes scream *WRONGDOER!* like nobody's business.

I climb back onto the street bare-chested, knock-kneed, and a little less nappy-headed. The only clothes I'm still wearing are my multi-colored silk boxers and my shoes. The wind feels like it's blowing through me. The digital display on my watch reads *2:22 a.m.*

I tell myself I can get away with just looking like a guy out for a late run or an early, early morning jog. I convince myself that this is who I am now. It's always about the story you tell yourself.

I cross the road and start running on the shoulder facing traffic. There's no traffic, but if there was traffic, I'd be facing it. The cop lights, way back at the Plaid, seem like another person's story. Just in case there're cops hiding up here somewhere with their lights out, I try not to look like I'm running away from anything. I run all loose and limp-wristed like a law-abiding citizen. If I can get to the stoplight in the distance, I can get home.

With each kick of gravel the stoplight becomes more than just a faint hope. It becomes a yellow hazard. A red dot. A green light again. I make a promise to not do stupid shit anymore if I'm just given this one pass. I keep telling myself that I've never ran away from anything. Ever. Not even now. I'm just an early, early morning jogger *getting a good jump on the day.* I'm trying to sound whiter than shit in my head. I picture myself saying *My, my, the cold is such a great way to combat muscle inflammation.* It sounds like something Mr. Futcher, the P.E. teacher, would say while doing side bends. I'm trying to build a believable story. What kind of stories are Squeaky and Thowa caught in? Did Squeaky get got just around the side of the store? Did Thowa just punch that cop and keep running? Is that possible? I refocus on the green light in the distance. I push everything else out of my mind. The light goes yellow. I keep putting one foot in front of the next. It goes red. Keep my elbows bent and pumping at my sides. *Not too anxious*, I tell myself, *Don't look too anxious.*

I wonder if it will always be like this: just barely getting away, forever.

Real dogs are barking behind me.

Don't look back.

I focus on the squishhh-chhhh! that my wet Converse are making on the gravel.

White circles form under the stoplight I'm running toward.

It's a car coming my direction. But I don't even think about veering off course.

Squishhh-chhhh! I'm just an early, early morning jogger.

Squishhh-chhhh!

Later this will just be another story.

Squishhh-chhhh!

Fine night for a jog, Officer.

Squishhh-chhhh!

I'm not so much squinting into the growing headlights as I am smiling.

Squishhh-chhhh!

Ready for them.

Squishhh-chhhh.

Ready for all of it.
Ready for a new...
Wait.
Is that *Old-E's* Caprice?

Landscaping Keepsakes
and the Eternal Under-Bed

Everybody was gathered around Aunt Joobie's opened grave, staring down the hole that looked deeper than six feet. The casket had dulled under the dirt over time. Shovel markings from various years' unburyings, scratched the once-glossy veneer. The lid of the upper half of the casket was propped open, revealing the insides off-white lining and button divots. The coffin looked welcoming, all open and empty like that.

"Always had to be the center of attention," Young Buck's mother said from behind the tombstone, steam rising from her words and disappearing overhead.

Young Buck winced, but knew what his mother meant. He knew she'd somehow put their differences aside and managed to make friends with her sister-in-law. And then the bullet meant for Uncle Melville hit Joobie instead, and Buck's mother just couldn't forgive the woman for destroying her brother's sanity by dying.

Young Buck was still fairly young when his aunt died, so the only solid memories he had of Joobie were of her funeral. Mostly of her framed pictures on the empty casket. After the funeral, his older sister, Ivy, had asked Buck, "How long's Joobie going to be hiding under the bed?"

His mother had overheard the question and slipped Ivy some more of her pills. Buck didn't have an answer for Ivy back then. And he didn't now. He wondered if it was comforting or scary to think of Joobie eternally waiting to be found under some box spring like that. Young Buck would have to ask Ivy whose bed she thought Joobie was under the next time she called collect.

"That girl sure did know how to ruin a holiday," Grandma P said, from the side of Joobie's grave, her eyes following the uneven dirt walls down.

"Shoot, you're telling me," Uncle Chappy said over the curve of his cigarette. "Couldn't have an open bowl of anything without her spiking it. That girl knew I was AA. Knew I loved me some egg nog. 'Come on, Joobie,' I'd say while she was tipping that poison in."

"Oh, you know you right," said Grandpa P's ground-up voice. "Figures she'd pick Thanksgiving to haunt this year. Turkey getting all cold on the table and..."

"You know you all plumb lost your minds?" said Cousin Couscous.

Couscous was a couple years older than Young Buck, just visiting from college out east. Over the years, she'd grown less tolerant of everyone standing around this gravesite begrudging her dead mother. She felt her family members *tsking* her. But it was her mother. Wasn't it her right to mourn the most? And here they were, mourning cyclically, like some ridiculous hurricane that never stopped stirring shit up.

Couscous shook her head and frowned at each of them. "The ability for a ghost to ruin a family gathering is a pretty inaccurate barometer for the amount they're actually missed."

"What do you remember about your mama?" Young Buck asked her.

"I remember her dying just when I needed her most. I remember Daddy drinking and crying all over the furniture. I remember Top Ramen every day. I remember wondering what it would have been like if that shooter hadn't missed. If Daddy had been the one shot instead."

Couscous looked down. "What do you remember, Buck?"

Young Buck looked at the ground, not the grave, but the point where the grass crept just short of it. There were red and yellow leaves circling around his ankles. Some blew into the hole and fluttered down. The breeze smelled clean, like fresh hung linen on a sagging line. Buck realized how accepting he'd become of his Uncle Melville perpetually stealing Aunt Joobie's ring out of her casket, crying on it for days, then insisting it be buried again. Now

Young Buck associated the holidays with the sound of shovels and soil falling on wood.

If they'd had Joobie's ring now, someone could've sealed that grave in viewing glass to make the perfect landscaping keepsake: a vertical zoo cage to keep Joobie's ghost in. That way Uncle Melville could come back as much as he liked to spend time with the ring, talk to it from up top, and not have to bother to dig a fresh hole every year just to be alone with it.

"Where you think your Daddy's gone?" Grandpa P asked Cousin Couscous.

"Probably where he always does—hitching the 5 South."

"Just glad we had her cremated," Chappy said. "Imagine the mess Melville could make otherwise."

"Why the hell do we keep burying that ring?" Grandpa P said.

"Let's just go get it," nodded Grandma P, "before Mr. Mike notices this pile of earth here."

"You right," Grandpa P muttered. "Let's go get that boy."

The wind blew more leaves, red and yellow, into the grave where Joobie's body never was, not even her ashes.

Young Buck nodded to himself.

Everybody turned and started walking away.

Couscous kneeled down and wiped her eyes. She stared down at the coffin and its open lid. She pushed her hand into the loose soil at her feet, squished it around, let it rain down onto the button-divot white linen. Then she eased one leg and the other over the side and slowly started climbing into her mother's empty grave. To mourn like only she could. To feel the satin and the divots and the emptiness surround her.

Real-Life Story Problem

"Everybody get the fuck down!" yelled Franklin.

And for a minute, everybody in the mall's third-story food court paused.

The cash registers went silent.

"I said get the fuck down!" Franklin repeated and pulled the air gun from his waistband and fired one shot at the spinning ceiling fans high above. His voice was louder than the discharge. The air gun had no orange tip. The air gun just looked like a gun gun.

An overhead light exploded from the pellet.

The blonde who worked at Hot-Dog-On-A-Stick and who wore a vertically-striped red, white, yellow, and blue pillbox hat, with sleeveless shirt and matching shorts—who had adorable dimples, and wore *Obituary Autumn* lip gloss by Revlon—got the fuck down.

The heart-of-gold metalhead with the multi-colored rubber bands extending from his goateed, scarred-up, butt-chin broke all four tines off his plastic fork mid-orange-chicken stab, choked momentarily on his tongue ring, and got the fuck down.

The ice skaters on the frozen rink two stories below, oblivious to the food court proceedings, side-slid into one another and shared last year's pictures of their families—fingering quickly over the dull moments on their smartphones, saying, "Aren't they precious?"

Or saying, "Take a good look at what I put up with."

Or saying, "Are we playing Red Light, Green Light or something? Because if we are, I'm sitting this one out."

A teenage girl, lacing up her first pair of brown rental skates on the red carpeted bench-seat, said, "Oh, you always have to be so fucking different, don't you?" to no one, and everyone, and skated out onto the ice rink, deliberately crashing into every couple. Falling on the cold medium to make snow angels where snow didn't exist, ever, and said, "Look at me, Daddy, I finally made it."

And her Daddy smiled the fuck down, through two vertical bars of the third-story guardrail, while crouching under the speckled food court table, thinking that if he died right then and there he'd die unfulfilled, still pining for the remaining three quarters of his strawberry Orange Julius just inches above him.

A blind man's service dog barked twice to signal to his master to "Get the fuck down!" But the blind man thought it was the signal for "Run your fucking ass off!" and dashed off at top speed, and top-sided over the guardrail, and dangled from the creases of his fingers high above the ice rink.

Franklin looked around him.

He fired a second plastic pellet into the flip-top lid covering of the escalator Emergency Stop Button. The lid cracked, but the stairs kept disappearing into the under-flooring—hungry to devour little fingers, and toes, and unsuspecting children.

Franklin fired another pellet from his air gun into the C in Cinnabon, and it rained electric sugar and purple sparks of passion onto Tiffany and Briana's Aqua-Net-ed hair. Their stylish fumes caught flames. The girls stopped, dropped, and rolled—coming out mostly unscathed but unable to smell cinnamon ever again without crying on the shoulders of others.

Franklin's next shot jammed in the gun's chamber.

The mall's sprinkler system erupted, having been activated by Tiffany and Briana's still-off-gassing hair.

The giant pretzels began getting soggy on the counters.

Franklin went to one knee and pulled the air gun's magazine, and checked the CO_2 cartridge. He knew he shouldn't have purchased the cheapest piece of shit Amazon had to offer.

Curtis, the armed security guard who had initially gotten the fuck down, was now getting the fuck back up again. He was only two years Franklin's senior and crouched thirty feet to Franklin's left. They both hailed from Grant High. They both grew up listening to Tupac. Unlike Franklin, Curtis had a baby at home that his fiancée would be putting down any minute. Nobody puts a baby the fuck down. Babies get put down, gently.

Curtis had a family. Franklin had a family. Everybody has a family. Families make the world go round. Where is your family right now?

Eyewitnesses report that when your momma got the tweet that the mall was under attack, she ran all the way from Marshall's to Spencer's, to binge-fantasize on Chippendale posters. I guess that's how your momma gets the fuck down.

In the third-story food court, Curtis pulled his self-purchased sidearm and aimed it at Franklin. Curtis was in a squat-stance so obscene that it looked like he was hovering over an invisible toilet in an invisible Honey Bucket. It was the only stance he could remember from a lifetime of movie viewing and the four-hour training class he'd taken a week prior.

Franklin turned his head to the left after clearing the jam in the air gun—one knee floored, one knee upright.

The metalhead with the heart of gold found a crack that looked like Jesus fogging over on the tile flooring to the side of his half-smashed cheek.

The daddy, still under the table, finally decided to make a move, for his Orange Julius.

Mid-squat, Franklin locked eyes with Curtis. Curtis locked eyes with Franklin. Curtis's eyes squinted. Franklin's eyes squinted. They raised their guns in unison.

Now stop.

Rotate the camera.

How does this end?

This isn't really a story. This is a problem.

Solve it.

Background considerations for your equation:

Both boys are natives from the planet Who-Gives-A-Fuck, but Curtis only visits during the holidays, and Franklin still lives there full-time. Neither has a father to speak of. Neither has a point of reference. Neither likes algebra. Both are sure shots. Both drink chocolate milk.

Knowing what you now know, who spoke first? Curtis or Franklin? The bullet or the pellet? *a* or *b*?

Solve using the Pythagorean Theorem. You are a magic-matician. Inject yourself into the equation, solve for Franklin.

Now solve for Curtis.

Now solve for your momma.

Now solve for the blind man hanging above the ice rink. Did you forget about him?

Who incurred more damage?

Add an unpopular variant. Consider culture. Consider media.

Solve for the Mediterranean: $a^2 + b^2 =$ Gyro, Gyro, Gyro!

Write your answer in bullet holes from a historical distance.

Divide your heart rate by your respirations and stay present. Stay palpable. Go to college.

Time's up.

Put down your pencil and pick up your sidearm. Add darkness. Encapsulate in parentheses. Extrapolate ad nauseam. Show your work for full credit.

Now stand to the side of your eraser marks and spent lead, and tell me, what the fuck happened?

Finding Timo

(Six Party Games for Late Night Postmortem)

Game 1 – Hide 'N Seek 'N Hide Again

When it's Uncle Timo's turn to hide, he fades quickly into the autoimmune disease while we all count to ten thousand and keep counting. We hold our breath between the numbers. We count at different speeds, trying to find the rhythm that makes everything right again. But Timo dies anyway. Everybody says it wasn't his time yet. Uncle Robbie says that if Timo can go out like that, then God's a little bitch.

We all nod in agreement.

Uncle Robbie says that Timo never stopped smiling. Even right up 'til the end, when he barely had the energy to. Even when it was difficult for him to breathe and his facial bones were becoming his face, Timo kept smiling.

We put one-thousands between the numbers as we count, "One one-thousand, two one-thousand, three one-thousand," so we don't go too fast. So we don't lose pace.

After the funeral, Grant says, "That's why you don't want to be such a good person. That's a sure way to have God make an example outta you," just trying to say something profound while sucking up to Uncle Robbie. He's always sucking up.

"I'm going to count ten," Uncle Robbie tells Grant, "and then I'm gonna to punch you in the chest."

But Uncle Robbie doesn't punch him. Instead he takes a deep breath and holds it. I picture him counting in his head to a number that will bring his brother back.

I take a deep breath and keep counting, too. *One hundred and ten one-thousand; one hundred and eleven one-thousand.*

When Uncle Timo is lowered into the ground I wonder if I'll see him again, if there's a place like that.

Game 2 – Edward Forty-Hands and the One-Inch Punch

After Uncle Timo's funeral, we don't talk about it.

We act tough because we're angry.

We drink and keep drinking.

Uncle Robbie is already half-drunk before the rest of us even get started. He's trying to catch us all up.

We're drinking Malt Liquor from forty-ounce bottles in Darren's parents' basement. I'm standing against the brick wall of the sublevel garage, next to the weight bench. The plastic that surrounds the cheap plates on the barbell is broken and showing the concrete underneath. The wall is cold against my shoulders and the backs of my legs. There are cracks in the concrete at my feet, cracks in the wall at my back.

We're playing Edward Forty-Hands without the duct tape. You have to have the fortitude to hold on to that bottle and keep drinking. In theory, you could let go of the forty, or stop drinking at any time, but we don't, we won't. At least I won't. Because if I stop chugging, Uncle Robbie has promised to get me in the stomach with that one-inch punch of his. He's standing only inches in front of me, encouraging me to keep drinking.

I've seen Robbie use that punch on the heavy bag hanging in the corner. The bag that's all saggy and beat-up in the middle. The punch created a ripple so deep that I thought the flooring above our heads was going to come down and bury us, right there in Darren's parents' basement-garage. I wondered what that punch would do to a person. I'd never seen Robbie *really* hit somebody, but I know he could. I know it would hurt. If he punches me for giving up on chugging the forty in my hand, I know it will be out of love. But it'll still hurt.

Robbie stands directly in front of me. "Come on," he says, "you can do it."

57

This is our idea of motivation, our endurance training.

Uncle Robbie says, "Don't let that bottle down, man."

And I don't.

Robbie teaches us about limits; that there aren't any.

"Don't tip that forty down, Homie," Robbie says.

I'm thinking he probably won't use that one-inch punch on me if I stop chugging, but I don't stop chugging because (more than anything) I don't want to disappoint Robbie right now. We all miss his brother, Timo. But the truth is that Robbie misses him the most. I've never seen him so upset and trying so hard to hide it, and I don't want to find out what happens if I stop drinking.

I watch the bubbles travel up through the piss-colored Malt Liquor until the liquid disappears and there's nothing but white fizz bubbles popping inside the bottle's neck.

When I lower the empty bottle, Uncle Robbie slaps the top of my shoulders twice with his hard palms and pulls me in for a hug and slaps me twice more on the back. I count each slap. They feel good. My stomach is sour, but my heart is full.

Game 3 – One-Car Tetris

We climb into Uncle Robbie's Chrysler LeBaron—one of the smaller, early '90s models—parked in front of Darren's parents' house.

In the front seat is Uncle Robbie (driving), Darren (who's Robbie's only real nephew here) sitting shotgun, and Justin squeezed between them. In the back seat is me (behind Darren), Grant (sitting back-bitch), and T-Dog (behind Uncle Robbie). Wendy's sitting on T-Dog's lap. Her hair's pulled back in a blue bandana. Her knees are crammed into the back part of Robbie's seat. It feels like we shouldn't fit.

We all have half-full forties in our hands with the caps on. Uncle Robbie's is between his knees. He backs out of the driveway and the tires on the LeBaron's passenger side miss the easement and fall off the curb, one at a time, and we're all shaken around. Wendy looks like a bobble-head doll as each wheel comes down, swaying on T-Dog's lap, her torso going the opposite direction of her curls.

Wendy smiles huge. T-Dog smiles huger.

We pull away from the house.

The streets are dim all around us. Every second streetlight is burned out. When Uncle Robbie looks in the rearview mirror, I can see his teeth. The way he pulls his upper lip back. It makes his face not quite a grimace, not quite a smile.

"Let's get this fucking night on the rooooooad," he howls.

He turns the knob on the radio and the six-by-nine speakers fill the insides of the car with that Zapp and Roger's song *I Want to be Your Man*.

I mouth the words to myself, because my singing voice sucks. Timo's voice didn't suck. His voice was smooth like Marvin. Timo's not here now.

"Timo loved this song," Uncle Robbie says while bobbing his head.

I feel Grant elbow me in my side to get at the cigarette pack in his pants. The car lurches forward and slows. Lurches forward and slows. Like Robbie's counting with the gas pedal.

Justin cracks his forty open, up front, between Uncle Robbie and Darren.

Robbie turns to him and says, "You better not spill any of that shit, Homie." He keeps going hard on the gas and easing off. Justin puts his cap back on.

The chorus of the Zapp and Roger's song fills the tiny cracks between the seven of us. Justin's Newport smoke fills our lungs. The malt liquor sloshes in our bottles, promising to fill something bottomless that we don't know how to share, so we won't talk about. We are a tight pack, packed tightly.

Game 4 – Urban Pac-Man

It's late enough that the streets are mostly abandoned. We drive past the car lots on 122nd, the cop shop on Glisan Street, the MAX line at Burnside, the library by the titty bar. Nobody spills a drop on Uncle Robbie's upholstery. Or if we do, we wipe and wipe and pray it dries unnoticed and won't admit it to anyone. Ever.

"How you feel about a little Pac-Man?" Robbie says.

He steers the LeBaron so that from inside it appears like the front of the car's hood is consuming the white dashes on the street. Each dash is another pellet. We're Pac-Man. We eat things.

"Look at me. I'm *Miss* Pac-Man," Wendy says, opening and closing her mouth on the air at the backside of the Robbie's headrest.

"Where, the fuck, are those ghosts?" Uncle Robbie says under his breath towards the windshield.

He bunches his face up.

He laughs.

We all laugh.

None of us want to laugh, not even Robbie, but we need to.

Uncle Robbie puts both of his hands on the steering wheel and swerves the LeBaron over the double-yellow lines. We're half in the northbound and half in the southbound lanes of traffic. We're Pac-Man on a killing spree; when all the ghosts blink the same color. It's late enough that we only have to watch out for cops and other Pac-Men coming in the opposite direction. Traffic's clear as far as we can see. No one but us gobbling power pellets out here.

I wonder if this is what the day after the end of the world would be like. I wonder if it would be this peaceful. I wonder if Timo's laughing his ass off somewhere right now at how ridiculous it all is.

Grant hands me the stub of his cigarette, and I take a drag before tossing the butt out the window. The butt sparks on the street and fades behind us. Grant lights another one.

Wendy is leaning forward on T-Dog's lap, her curly hair pulled back in that blue bandana, her eyes transfixed out the front windshield, her mouth still opening and closing in slow-motion like she's eating the solid yellow line on the road.

"Where the fuck *are* those ghosts at," Uncle Robbie says again. He's staring out the windshield, not really looking at anything, kind of looking beyond everything. He tips his forty with one hand at the side of his mouth and swallows hard.

I look out the side window and wonder what Timo's doing right now. I picture him riding cross-legged on top of the car, singing *I Want You* by Marvin Gaye. It feels possible.

In real life, Timo would never ride on the top of a car.

In the afterlife, you do whatever you want.

Game 5 – Old-E Pro-Am Off-Roading

Uncle Robbie brings his forty-ouncer down from his mouth and spills a little, and either doesn't notice, or doesn't care—shit, it's his ride, he'll spill if he wants to. He puts the bottle back in his lap and turns the steering wheel hard to the left. The LeBaron fishtails and shoots forward into a cluster of side streets off the main road.

He lets off the gas and straightens the car so it doesn't jump the curb.

"No hands," Robbie says with one arm out the window and the other accidentally backhanding Justin across the left side of his face.

Justin says, "Ugh," and rubs his cheek.

Robbie grabs the steering wheel again, and accelerates, and we're all forced back like sci-fi rocket propulsion. Wendy head-butts T-Dog with her giant puff of curls. T-Dog puts his hand to his forehead, trying to rub away the hair in his face, and elbows Grant in the shoulder. Grant nearly swallows his cigarette. The lit cigarette glances off of his teeth and lands between us.

"Shit," Grant says while batting and rummaging at our thighs.

"What the fuck is going on back there?" Uncle Robbie says.

The LeBaron cuts hard to the right and jumps a curb into somebody's front yard. Robbie faces forward with the jolt and regains control and steers hard to the left.

"Got it," Grant says. He holds up the cigarette, just before we're all thrown to the right.

It's the centrifugal motion of a Tilt-a-Whirl.

"Whooo weee!" Uncle Robbie yells out the driver's window like a kid on The Scrambler. He leans harder into the steering wheel as the LeBaron cuts grass cookies out of somebody's front lawn. Grant's almost in my lap. Soil is squeezed out from under the tires and is shooting up and raining down around us.

We come to a skidding stop in the middle of the fourth or fifth circle of freshly uprooted earth, and Grant looks over his shoulder at me. The knuckles of his finger and thumb are going white because he's clasping his cigarette so hard in front of my face, all smiles and sweat. I push him back to the middle seat.

We're parked in the front yard of a house with a big picture window and a TV on inside. The lights make the whole room look like a time machine changing colors before it blinks out of existence. There's the silhouette of a man in a t-shirt and a woman with a ponytail, standing in the middle of the large window. I'm hoping they just disappear.

Uncle Robbie says, "Isn't that some shit?" to nobody in particular.

"We gotta get out of here," Darren says, looking over Justin at his uncle.

"Get out of here? What you in such a rush for, man?" Uncle Robbie says.

Darren leans his head to the side and points at the silhouette of the couple in the window. His hand is shaking a little.

Uncle Robbie looks at his nephew. Gives a long sigh. Turns his head to look at the couple.

"Oh, that," he says, sounding bored. "Fuck them."

Grant is puffing like mad at the stub of his cigarette while trying to rub away the burn mark it made in the LeBaron's upholstery.

"They can wait a minute," Robbie says calmly. "Hey, is everybody okay?" he asks. He takes his time looking at each one of us. He dusts off Justin's shoulder. He looks over at Darren again. When Uncle Robbie looks back at Grant, Grant stops wiping at the seat and smiles stiffly.

Everything slows down for a moment. I can feel myself breathing without trying to. How often does that happen? I can hear my heart whooshing in my ears. Time has a way of getting weird with Uncle Robbie; it goes at his pace.

I look back at the couple in the window. They're still there. The man looks like he's yelling in sign language now. The woman's tugging on his arm like she's trying to pull him away from an ocean with a shark in it. Uncle Robbie steps out of the LeBaron and stands in their front yard, in the middle of the grass circle he just made with the car.

He looks down and says, "My fucking shoes are muddy now."

He looks at the window with the couple in it and yells, "What the fuck's your problem?"

He puts his arms out to his sides and holds them there, his palms facing the house like he wants to give it the most menacing hug ever.

Pointing to the LeBaron, he says, "Look how dirty my ride is, man."

The couple just stands there.

The man puts his arms down. The woman stops pulling. Time stops for them, too. I can feel it.

Uncle Robbie gets back in the LeBaron and slams the door. "Let's go to the mountains," he says. "Fuck this place."

Game 6 – Blackout Gorge Bingo

Before leaving the Portland city boundaries, Grant wants to go home, so he's dropped off at the next stoplight, "...for acting like a little bitch about it."

Wendy has to be somewhere in the morning so Robbie drops her off at her front door (parking in the street, not on the grass) and tells her to have a good night and that it was enjoyable spending time with her.

After she gets out, he turns to the backseat and says, "If you boys don't know chivalry by now, you better figure it the fuck out."

Justin comes back to sit between T-Dog and me since now there's only five of us.

We drive through Gresham and Troutdale and get more forties out of a cardboard box in the trunk and drink them on the way to nowhere. We hit the Old Historic Hwy, outside of Corbett where it's all mountains, with the bottles between our thighs. Trees appear in the headlights and disappear into the darkness around us.

While I'm counting forward, time is counting backwards.

None of us ask where we're going. None of us cares.

Maybe it's Multnomah Falls that Robbie's heading to. The last time we were out there we made a game of seeing who could hold onto the underside of the tracks the longest while the train roared overhead.

"It's therapeutic to scream at the top of your lungs, and not be able to hear your own voice," Uncle Robbie had said. "That's just science. You start to realize that the *you* inside *you* probably isn't who you think it is."

Timo was still alive back then, when Robbie'd said that, but Timo hadn't actually been with us. He never seemed to have the angst we had.

Robbie said that Timo had worked all that angst out when they were younger and now he'd earned the right to just kick back and laugh and sing about shit. He said Timo didn't have to test his limits because he already knew them, he already knew they didn't exist. He said that's why he sang so well.

I pull my forty from between my legs and crack the cap in the back seat of the LeBaron, and don't spill a drip. The malt liquor's warm, but it doesn't matter, it's just filler. We swerve along the Historic Hwy, and Robbie takes his hands off the steering wheel. He accelerates into the darkness.

Trees come in and out of the headlights.

Ice-T's *New Jack Hustler* is playing through the LeBaron's six by nines.

Ice raps about his posse and bumping his sound and laughing over freshly cracked forties.

The LeBaron drifts into the oncoming lane, like we're playing Pac-Man again, but we're not. We only see trees where the headlights pierce the darkness. Trees and road signs and the ledge come and go. Everything's narrower and darker out here. Nobody but us exists. Maybe nobody ever did. We're gliding off course again. Always.

Before the car hits the gravel of the opposite shoulder Uncle Robbie slowly guides us back into the right lane.

"You think you have control in this life?" Uncle Robbie asks.

We don't know if it's rhetorical.

"You think any of us has control?" he says. "You think Timo had control?"

Nobody knows what the right answer is.

Robbie shuts off the headlights. We float over a dark cloud.

Ice-T raps about low education and pitbulls and hearts like nitro.

The headlights come back on, and we're in the oncoming lane again. I'm smiling. I'm always smiling when I'm the most afraid.

T-Dog and Justin are just silhouettes beside me. Justin's hands are ringing his forty's neck. Up front, Darren takes a pull on his malt liquor, and I know it's warm. Like mine. I can taste it.

We all know this is just another test. Everything's just another test, just another game.

"*Tests are what make you who you will be later.*" It's something Timo used to say. I wonder if I'm passing this test. His test.

"You damn right Timo had control," Uncle Robbie says to himself, to the windshield, maybe to us. "Because he knew that you have to give up control, to overcome it."

Uncle Robbie turns the radio off. The tires hum on the asphalt below us.

He twists the headlights off again.

He takes his hands off the steering wheel, leans his head back, and looks at the upholstered ceiling of the LeBaron. Uncle Robbie's hands are interlocked behind his head now, like he's on vacation or something. At best he's driving with his knees, by Braille. I get the feeling his eyes are closed, so I close my eyes. I start counting under my breath.

"One one-thousand, two one-thousand, three one-thousand." I count so low that the words barely exist.

I assign one one-thousand for each rivet in the road, for each nod of my head, for each upcoming tree I picture stopping us, out here in the forest. Forever.

I listen to the sound of the LeBaron's tires on the asphalt as we increase speed. Hear the crunch of the rubber finding gravel.

"Seven one-thousand."

I hear the silence of tires finding asphalt again.

When I open my eyes I think I see Uncle Robbie wiping his face with the back of one hand. I don't know if his other hand's on the wheel or not. I close my eyes again.

"Eleven one-thousand, twelve one-thousand, thirteen one-thousand..."

The Uncomfortable Augmentations
of Earl Sneed Sinclair

Franklin, Rasheed, and I found the used Earl Sneed Sinclair costume on Amazon, for cheap. Well, actually, Franklin found it, and he said it was cheap and we trusted him, so we pooled our money together and bought it. He said that Earl was from the TV sitcom, *Dinosaurs*. How it was this groundbreaking '90s fad that his dad used to be obsessed with.

Franklin paraphrased the concept of *Dinosaurs* like this, "Imagine the sitcom *Roseanne* taking place on Pangea, only with animatronics."

But I couldn't, so I Googled it.

"Those things are pretty fucking creepy," Rasheed said over my shoulder about the YouTube clip we'd found.

"Whatever," said Franklin.

In the clip, the baby dinosaur—whose first name is literally *Baby*—was hitting his spoon on his Stone Age highchair and screaming, "KNOCK THE MAMA!"

"What the hell does that mean?" I said. "Knock the mama?"

"Wow, television's come a long way," said Rasheed.

"Knock the mama?" I couldn't stop saying it.

"No, dude, it's not *Knock* the Mama, it's *Not* the Mama," said Franklin.

"What?"

"It's like early '90s women's lib shit, man," said Franklin.

"What?"

"Yeah," said Franklin all whispery, mostly to himself, closing his eyes and nodding slowly, "that's the magic of a Jim Henson-Walt Disney marriage right there, friend. It's all about family."

A week later, the Earl Sneed Sinclair costume arrived at our house. It was stuffed into two old, taped-together, refrigerator boxes.

Earl was the patriarch of the *Dinosaur* family. He was a megalosaurus. I guess. The costume came with a red flannel shirt sewn over a white tee. It didn't have pants. Franklin said that dinosaurs didn't need pants. I wondered why they needed shirts.

The thing had a tail and was awkwardly huge. Franklin put the costume on first and walked around the apartment in it. The tail knocked the remote and ashtray off of the coffee table when he turned. The hips grazed the hallway walls he wandered down. It knocked over our only house plant from the living room speaker.

Then Franklin made Rasheed put it on.

Then me.

It felt dank and too warm inside. I could see how somebody could get claustrophobic after only a few minutes in there. There was a lot more rubber than I thought there would be, probably for cleaning purposes. There wasn't any kind of little head fan or anything. I wondered how porous rubber was. I wondered how many other people's old sweat I was encased in. I figured we'd have to pull straws to see who had to wear it out in public.

"People actually wore this costume while filming?" I said from inside Earl. My voice echoed around me.

"No, man. Those were robot puppets. *Animatronics*. This suit was strictly for theme park purposes, it just never made it there," Franklin said while he pawed distractedly at the outer material.

The next morning, we found Franklin already wearing the megalosaurus costume. He was in the kitchen making breakfast for us. But that shit wasn't made to cook in. He almost caught Earl's hands on fire. There were charred marks on the thumbs. Earl only had four digits on each hand to begin with. Rasheed and I had to clean the pancake mix and uncooked eggs off of Earl's flannel shirt and puffy body while Franklin kept saying, "I'm sorry, Earl. I'm sorry," from still inside the thing.

"Why were you already in this?" I said.

"Just wanted to be ready for our big day, buddy." But he didn't sound like Franklin in there. He sounded goofier.

"Did you put this on last night?" I asked.

"N-no."

Outside, the three of us climbed into an Uber van going to Pioneer Square. Franklin was still in Earl. The only way he fit was by lying diagonally across the middle bench seat and using seatbelt extenders. Rasheed sat on the bench seat behind him. I sat shotgun.

The Uber guy said, "This is my first prehistoric transport," and chuckled.

I just looked at him.

Franklin laughed. His laugh sounded different inside the costume. It wasn't just the echo that made it weird.

I was starting to think this dinosaur costume wasn't going to earn us any money, like Franklin had promised. After all, Pioneer Square wasn't Times Square or Disneyland or Vegas. And the outfit was too freaky, too outdated and unknown, too not-purple-enough if we were going for the kid angle, and too unmarred for the ironic postmodern motif. I was starting to think it was just Franklin, living out some childhood dream in there, on our dime.

I thought I kept hearing him say, "Papa," but it could have been, "Putt-Putt," or, "What? What?" Earl's head muffled a lot of enunciation. Who knows, maybe Franklin was just struggling to breathe.

And, just like I thought, down at The Square people weren't exactly lining up to pay for photos with Earl Sneed Sinclair. The few little kids that walked by with their parents didn't even know who he was. They seemed scared. The teenagers down there tried stepping on his tail. And no adults were asking if it was okay to snap pictures of Earl for a dollar, they were just doing it, from a distance, and steering clear of our donations can. After three hours downtown, the only action Earl got was a slow dance with a homeless dude, an onslaught of belly bumps from a group of already drunken frat guys, a little tumble down the brick stairs, and a cop who kept asking us for our costume license. Is a costume license even a thing? I'm pretty sure he was just making sure Earl wasn't some kind of terrorist bomb.

Once we got back home, Rasheed and I worked at getting some of the stuck gum out of Earl's flannel.

"That was some fall!" Franklin said, recalling his descent down the square's stairs, as I picked at a particularly stubborn pink wad.

"Might be easier to clean if you just took the thing off, Franklin," I said.

"I'm good, man. It kind of takes a while to come out of character, you know?"

"No. I don't know," I said.

I went to bed.

I got up late the next day. I didn't see Franklin or the Earl costume at all before leaving for my nightshift at the windows factory.

All night, I placed windows against other windows, frame to frame, like rows of tightly packed translucent dominoes. I tied them in place to the slats on the trailer walls with trucker knots. I worked with mostly illegal immigrants. They worked harder than me. I drank cups of coffee during my lunch break. I thought about how this job was going nowhere. I thought about how the windows I tied down saw other parts of the country while I stayed put. I wondered if it was healthy for me to be working nights and thinking so much.

When I got home the next morning, Earl looked like he was trying to set himself on fire at the stove again.

"Dude, careful!" I said.

"No, it's cool," Franklin's voice said from inside Earl's head. He turned around and held his palms out to me.

I could see he'd made cuts below the costume hands so that he could use his real hands while still wearing the thing. When Franklin turned back to the stove, I noticed a row of safety pins holding closed a homemade flap on Earl's butt region that wasn't there the last time I saw him. A tube exited Earl's crotch to what looked like a partially filled urine bag taped around his thigh.

Franklin took the pan off the stove and dumped some of the scrambled eggs into a bowl. They were the same color as the pee in the bag that was taped around his leg. I wondered if Franklin was going to try to eat the eggs with Earl's head still on. I hoped he didn't plan on trying to cut a mouth hole while still wearing it. I hoped he wouldn't ask me to cut the hole for him.

"Help yourself," Franklin said while nodding at the pan of eggs in his hand. I hated the way his voice sounded in there.

"Hey, buddy," I said, "can we talk about something?"

He put the pan down on the stove and turned back to me. I was face to face with Earl's ever-grinning, gap toothed, stupid mouth. I wondered how hard it would be to just rip Earl's head right off of his body. I wanted to see what facial expressions Franklin was making under there. It made communication just one step away from texting.

Was he fucking with us? Was all of this funny to him? Or was it really as sad as it seemed?

"I know what you're gonna say," Franklin said, Earl's head bowing and nodding as he spoke. "And you're right." One four-fingered hand scratched at Earl's leg. "I know I've been hogging Earl, man," he said. "But Jay, I think I can make it right. I think you're really gonna like what I found for you on Craigslist. Do you remember the Baby character?"

The Third Bullet

There are things you'll learn from books full of acronyms, whose titles are themselves acronyms, during your training to become an EMT-P (Emergency Medical Technician-Paramedic) on an ambulance. These books will teach you how to be more adept at foreseeing everything that can go wrong inside a person.

Take the PHTLS (Pre-Hospital Trauma Life Support) text, for example, and the many traumatic ways that people can spill out, detach, become crumpled. You'll learn that there are three ways you can die from a single explosion. Let's say that each explosion has three separate phases. Let's call these phases "bullets."

The first bullet is invisible. It's the wall of air rippling through your body; the hip-checking of all your hollow organs. Maybe this is when your lungs collapse, or maybe not—really that can happen at any stage. Remember your first kiss? The way it took the breath out of you? This is nothing like that.

The second bullet is more like an onslaught of bullets, more like a Gatling gun. It's broken concrete and rusty nails and tabletops and saltshakers and shattered glass and every piece of flying debris you can imagine, all coming at you and trying to merge. By now you know that not everything that seeks comfort in you is a good thing. This is the point where you're going to want to do that slo-mo limbo-yoga shit from *The Matrix* if you can. But this isn't the movies. And you're not that limber. If your heart's ever going to be impaled by a chopstick, it's probably now.

The third bullet (the last injury profile from an explosion) has to do with whatever your body lands in, on, or through once you stop flying through the air.

You are the third bullet.

It would be best if this part happened in one of those parkour gyms with a foam pit and a bunch of strong dudes ready to unbury your ass. But chances are it will happen in a place with brick-bricks instead of foam bricks. Chances are it won't ever happen, because this section of PHTLS is geared more toward the military, and you're not part of the military. You're just a guy on an ambulance. But you'll have to know how to treat these kinds of wounds, just in case.

When you're done with the PHTLS section, there'll be another class to take ASAP.

You'll get your PALS (Pediatric Advanced Life Support) certification to learn how to care for babies and kids in situations that babies and kids should never be in. You'll need your ACLS (Advanced Cardiac...) for other matters of the heart. You'll need more acronyms like PEEP and BP and JVD. You'll monitor SpO_2 levels in your CHF patients while holding their gaze and telling them that this CPAP mask will feel confining but will save them if they can embrace it. You'll pray it does, save them that is, while preparing for the next step in the algorithm.

You'll picture the worst-case scenario in every scenario until you get enough real-life experience to see the bigger picture. That picture will expand and contract. It will trick you into complacence. You'll count its respirations. You'll feel for a pulse. Sometimes it'll be there. Sometimes it's your imagination—just the faint beating of hope still warm from the environment.

Sometimes you'll come home after a shift and feel like you've made a difference. Other times you'll hug your kids tighter and worry more about everything that can happen to them.

One day you'll be in the ambulance, waiting for the next call to drop, and will start making up acronyms on your own, because there are never enough secret ways to convey information faster. There's no better way to reframe something than with fewer letters that mean much more. Plus, an acronym is a space saver. Just think of what's written on almost every gravestone and under the tattooed faces on biceps. Think of the space saved there. If you take the periods and capitalization away from *R.I.P.*, it's still a word. In this way, it's kind of like a backronym, but it's not.

You'll make up a backronym for F.A.I.T.H.—Falling and Ignoring the Heat—because you're an old dog at this. You'll make up one for C.O.M.P.A.R.T.M.E.N.T.A.L.I.Z.A.T.I.O.N., but it's too long to remember.

Because it might be a crime scene, you'll confirm your first Dead On Scene suicide while he's still hanging by his neck from a tree. It's in the section of town where all the street names are inspired by Lewis Carroll. There's Alice Lane. There's Mad Hatter Lane. There's Wonderland Park. The moon will be a giant smiling Cheshire Cat in the sky while you attach the EKG leads to the man's body, one at a time, from right to left, using the cooking mnemonic that corresponds to the colors of the electrode cords: salt, pepper, ketchup.

You put salt and pepper by the shoulders. Ketchup goes by the left hip.

You'll keep thinking about how this guy's knees are only inches above the ground. How his legs are folded behind him. You'll know that all he had to do to stay alive was stand up. You'll wonder why he didn't.

When you get back to the rig, your partner will say, "He really had to want it."

He'll say, "You'll get used to it after you've had enough of it."

He'll say, "Hey, let's grab something to eat. I'm hungry."

You'll stop using acronyms and backronyms and any other abbreviation on principle alone, because they all feel cheap—the bastardization of language, the poor man's aggrandizing of wit, the elitism of tribe. You'll always use full sentences when you text. You'll question life—what it means and all—and then realize how ridiculous that is.

One day your partner will tell you that maybe it won't be one thing, but the buildup of all these things—the chest pains and drunken traumas and fatal MVAs and dead babies—that end up emotionally weighing you down. He'll say you won't know until it happens, that it may be a run-of-the-mill call that finally breaks you.

He'll say, "Maybe it's as simple as a kid waving at you from the sidewalk with a melting orange-cream Popsicle running down his hand."

And you'll know that this sentence is more than hypothetical—it's too specific. And that'll make you wonder if this guy hasn't been doing this for too long. If he shouldn't get a car that needs a little TLC to work on, or more R&R in his off time, or an SSRI to make his outlook brighter. And the acronyms will be back, because really, they never left. You deal better with them. Shortening has its place. Abbreviation can be a virtue.

One day we'll be partners, you and I. Because everything changes. We've learned to expect the unexpected, and we know that consistency is the mother of complacency, but mostly it's because the company is short on paramedics. It's our second shift together. We'll be talking about music when a "Possible OD" call drops down the street.

When we get there, there's a fifteen-year-old female unresponsive and cyanotic, lying supine on the sofa. It's morning. The apartment's small. The lights are dim.

The girl's mom is holding her daughter, saying, "I was just talking to her before making breakfast."

There's the smell of eggs from the kitchen, heavy in the air.

The girl's mom says, "I think she was out all night with her friends."

You say, "We need to look at her," as you gently pry the girl out of her mother's arms. The mother stands a few feet away and watches. She sees everything. She *should* see everything. She'll have to interpret what it all means later.

The girl's eyes are open. Her pupils are fixed. Her gray T-shirt reads *OMG* in white blocky letters across her chest. She's apneic, but still warm. Her extremities are flaccid. There's vomit everywhere: in her hair, on the floor, sticking to her shirt, to the armrest.

I drop the medic kit and airway bag as you take the girl on the sofa in your arms and place her on the floor between the TV and the coffee table. And she feels as light as H.O.P.E. as you put her down. You feel for a pulse and start CPR. With the second compression, you feel her sternum separate from her ribs. It's a feeling you don't forget.

I attach the defibrillator pads and say, "Stop."

You check for a pulse at the carotid, look at the monitor, and say, "PEA," while beginning compressions again.

Her heart has electricity but isn't beating (good circuitry, bad generator).

There's the BVM.

The IV.

The ETT.

And even though this girl still isn't breathing, she also isn't R.I.P.

She still has a C.H.A.N.C.E.

But this mom's not OK. And you and I are EMT-Ps flipping through the acronyms. And are ourselves acronyms. And we're silently praying to an unknown G.O.D. to intervene. But there is no ETA for miracles here. There is no longer any rhythm on the monitor. No QT intervals. No QRS complex. No track marks or drug paraphernalia. No place for Narcan in the ACLS algorithm—but we talk about pushing it anyway. We speak in grunts and abbreviations.

The girl's mom says, "Speak English. What's happening?"

And you know we need to be clear here. We have to remove the periods from our letters for the words to make any sense. We know that some things are shortened for convenience, but some things aren't meant to be shortened. Ever.

I look at you, with your mouth hanging open. And I wonder what words you will choose when there's no right way to package them.

I watch your jaw tighten as you look from the girl's ashen face into her mom's hazel eyes. You're still doing chest compressions. Up and down. And this mom's daughter has a tube down her trachea. And her unbeating heart is being externally manipulated by the heels of your hands. And there are EKG pads on her chest. And your lips part as you say, "We're doing. Everything. We can, ma'am." And you mean it. And her mom nods, and cries harder, and doesn't believe you. And the smell of eggs from the kitchen still hangs in the air. And your lips begin moving, but they are not speaking. They are only silently counting their way from one to thirty and starting over again. Not because they have to, but because they've been trained to, because there's no way to make this easier. There's no way to make this right. There's a lump forming in your throat and rising to your eyes and clouding your vision. I know, because it's happening to me. It's happened to me. And now I'm the old guy. And you're the newbie. And we're in this together. We've always been in this together. And mostly we remember that. But sometimes we forget.

On the ambulance ride to the hospital, a firefighter is doing CPR while you administer another epi 1:10,000 bolus and an amp of sodium bicarb, and you blink back that lump in your throat, and swallow it down, and bury it somewhere inside. You don't have time for an epitaph.

At the ER, we transfer the girl from our stretcher onto the hospital bed and the nursing staff continues working the code. Until they don't. Until they call it, and the doc has to tell the mom that her daughter is dead, and there's nothing they can do about it.

He says, "Dead."

He doesn't say, "Passed on."

He doesn't say, "Gone to a better place."

The mom is given a chaplain to help her with the higher philosophical concepts.

We put fresh sheets on our stretcher; put the stretcher back into the ambulance.

It's not until we're back in the cab of the rig that I think about that third bullet of an explosion.

I think about all of us passing through this.

I think about the girl passing through this.

I think about the girl's mom passing through this.

Our pagers go off for an MVC up on Farmington. Cars are crashing into each other. We climb back into opposite sides of the rig. You turn the ignition. My mind automatically starts thinking about C-spine and TBIs, and OSS vs. backboards, and the entire anatomy of a car wreck. You hit the switch for the emergency overheads as we pull out of the ER bay and onto the street.

Inner Workings

Ralphie's eyes were light-blue-watery, the way they always got after the third pitcher. We'd started late anyway that night, and somehow it was already 1:30 in the morning, and most of the talent had gone home or never even shown up in the first place. It being a Thursday and all, none of this was really a surprise.

The only people left at Gruff's were the typical no-lifers. There was Tricia, the mid-forties bartender going on eighty-something in body and spirit. There were a couple of burnouts huddled in the far corner, checking the creases of old cellophane wrappers. There was Woo-Hoo, the seventy-year-old vet who kept trying to recruit Ralphie and me into the VFW—even though neither of us had ever been in the service. He'd yell out, "Wooo-Hoooo," every time Tricia bent under the bar to get him a fresh Pabst and he caught another peek of her drug-withered, cigarette-puckered cleavage.

The only real difference in Gruff's that night was the one person I haven't mentioned yet, the person everybody's eyes kept wandering back to. She had a pair of looker-legs attached to a treat-like torso and a face I imagined too beautiful to have found its way into this town, let alone this bar, on its own. Though, the truth is, I hadn't seen her face yet.

Legs sat in a tight white skirt and black thigh-highs. Her upper half was draped in a red leather jacket with frilly streamer adornments dangling from the undersleeves. She sat at the opposite side of the bar from Woo-Hoo, looking like a lady who sexy-crawled out of a Foreigner video and got up in your night cravings whenever she liked. At first I thought she could have been Tricia's younger, hotter kin, but they'd only been conversing through finger wags and head nods—tender/patron shorthand—and the kinship quickly became doubtful. I couldn't imagine what would've brought a stranger with legs like that into a place like this.

"I think I got a chance over there," Ralphie said, leaning over the tabletop and nodding to Legs at the bar. The lower part of Ralphie's beard was streaked off-white, like Rob Zombie's, from the beer suds gathering and popping there.

"Yup," I said. I loved Ralphie, wanted the best for him, wanted him to find a good woman, but it was fun seeing him get shot down, too—maybe not for Ralphie so much, but damn good entertainment for me. It was probably the only action we'd be getting that night anyway, if you could call "shame" action. In any case, I wasn't gonna discourage him.

"What's your game plan, Buddy?" I asked, staring at Ralphie's sizable beard hiding his baby face.

"I've been thinking a lot and reading a little," he said, "and I think I've figured it out."

I raised my pint and drained the last bit of ale at the bottom. I gave Ralphie a little head-tilt-half-wink and glanced at the empty pitcher. I tried not to look sad. "Figured what out, Buddy?"

"Well," said Ralphie, "seems to me that the young lady over there is in the need for some companionship."

"Mmm." I scratched at the four days growth on my neck and jawline. "*Your* companionship, you mean?" I asked.

"'Xactly," he said.

"How's that, Ralphie?"

I'd known Ralphie for damn near twenty years, ever since his family moved to Silence County and he joined our football team, the Runnin' Linesmen. Not much of a runner, but the boy had girth. Has girth. Hell of a blocker. Not so great at sealing the deal with the ladies, but a damn decent wingman.

"Way I see it," said Ralphie, "that girl is doing what we're doing, just passing the time until she meets the right person to help save her from herself."

"That's what we're doing?" I asked.

The last of the tiny froth bubbles were popping in Ralphie's beard, his face was shining over the grimy table, under the whiskey lights.

"Whooo-Hooooo!" Woo-Hoo yelled from the bar.

"You remember my Uncle Timmy?" Ralphie asked without outwardly acknowledging our vet's beer cry.

"Mm-hmm," I nodded.

"He sent me his prison reading list last summer."

Ralphie's uncle, Timmy Quarterlaine, had been sent stateside for carrying his 12-gauge into the Thompson's gas station and tying people up, years ago.

"Sounds educational," I said, managing to only chuckle a little.

"I guess so," Ralphie said, not catching my sarcasm. "They have a library in there and everything. He writes real good now, too, Sammy. Handwriting looks like a lady's, it's so pretty. Perfect circles above the 'i's and all."

"So Timmy writes like a woman, now?"

"You know what I mean, real easy to read. Ornamental in a way."

"Didn't know Timmy could read," I said only half joking.

"Well, they say incarceration is the mother of getting your shit together," said Ralphie with the sincerity of a librarian.

I nodded. "Is that what they say?"

I didn't know where Ralphie was going with all of this. I was even starting to lose interest in him getting shot down by those legs at the bar. He seemed too genuine with his theories, and Ralphie wasn't known for his theories. Maybe it was just the beer settling south in me, pulling me down. I wiped at my eyes. I didn't feel like getting up early the next morning. Didn't feel like doing much of anything.

"Lots of women out there love felons," Ralphie continued, beaming, as he passed his hand over the bar table. "Uncle Timmy says some women seek 'em out even, the felons I mean."

"You're not a felon, Ralphie."

"Yeah, but he says *he's* gotten a lot of writing practice that way, returning their letters and all. He's started reading Danielle Steele to get the inner workings of the female mind right in his own head.

Says his cellmate turned him on to it. And he swears it's the legal equivalent of crushing down ten dozen roses to a fine powder and making roofies out of 'em."

There was no doubt that last sentence was a direct Timmy quote. It had too much prison philosophy, too much twisted drug logic.

"*What* have you been reading?" I asked.

"Danielle Steele, just like Timmy," Ralphie said. "Hey, I've seen them lying around your mama's house, too."

"You've been reading my mama's books?"

"Whoooo-Hooooo," yelled Woo-Hoo from the bar up front. It was only his fifth Wooo-Hooo of the night. A little slow for him. He must have been nursing 'em before and was just now picking up steam.

"Inner workings, man," said Ralphie, not even turning in the direction of our very own, very excited, vet. "Those books hold the keys to the heart, Sammy." Ralphie's eyes locked on mine. Then they slowly shifted to where that woman with those legs sat sipping her liquor on the rocks. At least it started on the rocks. I imagined the rocks all melted over there. I imagined those legs felt real soft.

"So what's your plan, Ralphie?" I asked, nodding in her direction.

"Well, I've been sitting here thinking about that." He leaned back in his chair and scratched as his beard.

"And?"

"I'm gonna write her a note on this here napkin," he said, and pulled a cocktail nap up from under the table. He'd probably been balancing it on his thigh for who knows how long, trying to keep it clean and presentable.

"You got a pen, Shakespeare?" I said.

He half-stood, knees slightly bent like a Yeti considering a BM, and produced a white-stemmed pen with a black lid from his jeans' pocket. The back of that pen looked like it'd been chewed on pretty badly.

"Well, all right then," I said.

I could tell he'd been putting this together for a while—for days, maybe months—just waiting for the right time. The right girl. The right woman. Probably been honing in those perfect circles above his 'i's in his bed at night, like Uncle Timmy had done in his cell.

Ralphie looked down for a second. He tried to wipe a clean circle on the table with the end of his flannel sleeve. He smoothed out that napkin he'd been saving with the meaty sides of his hands, pulled the lid off that chewed up pen and laid it on the table.

Ralphie's hand shook a little as he wrote—looked like he was trying to take his time with it, but taking his time was only making it worse, what with all the uneven contours of the table grain and the stickiness. And the napkin he was writing on was not necessarily *of quality* in the first place. There were no consistent straight lines in the letters he was producing. I felt bad for Ralphie, for having come up with such a horrible plan.

I began feeling tired again. Probably just worked too hard, probably just imagining the two of us getting old and writing wobbly letters on napkins, together, after sunset, on disagreeable porches. I could taste the ale in the back of my throat needing food to coat it and take away the sour. But, damn it! Ralphie really was trying, biting his lower lip, attempting to write words coherently and all. Thinking he knew women's inner workings. I'm not saying I felt sentimental or anything, but goddamn; a man could have used a pitcher refill. Or maybe just fresh air. Or maybe...

"Whooo-Hooooo," Woo-Hoo yelled at Tricia's old bent-over cleavage swinging before him.

"We should just go, Ralphie," I said.

We had chainsaws to use as hands the next day. There'd be other nights to watch Ralphie get turned down by women with soft-looking legs. Plus, something about the way this woman sat didn't necessarily *invite* company. It could've been the way she crossed her thighs or the slight hunch of her shoulders. Or it could have been the fact that she reminded me of my ex, Laurie, somehow—and that just made me more tired. And here Ralphie was pouring himself out onto a napkin for nothing but disappointment, and I know, I know what you're thinking: that I was going as soft as those legs looked. But a part of me just wanted to save Ralphie from himself, from this embarrassment.

"I'm almost done," said Ralphie, all big-head-smiling. He drew a couple more circles above some of his 'i's and said, "That's it! It's perfect."

Ralphie laid the pen on the table, snatched the napkin up between his thumb and forefinger, and held it by the tiniest amount of corner, like it was some delicate artifact. The napkin hung all impotent in the air, already ashamed for him.

"That's okay, Ralphie. Maybe another day, buddy. Let's just go."

Ralphie lost his smile for a minute and got all serious. "I told you, Sammy, I know everything I gotta know. Maybe you could stand to watch and learn something."

"Well, alrighty," I said, suddenly finding the entertainment in it again, and leaned back on the rear two legs of my chair. "Have at it, buddy." I even gave him a facetious, descending, presenter's hand wave toward the direction he was bent on.

Ralphie seemed too focused on that note as he walked across the bar flooring to where Legs sat. He looked like a man staring at the fate lines in his own hand, about ready to walk straight into a hole that fell away into a fiery pit. 'Course, it could have just been the angle I was at.

I still couldn't see that woman's face. Figured it was beautiful, like Laurie's before Laurie left. Even if it wasn't, those legs were *the truth*, looked like they could tell a man something; like they'd be nice to fall into. I found myself batting another eyelash out of my eye. Didn't know a grown man could lose so many lashes. They always made my eyes water. I wondered how I still had any lashes left.

As Ralphie came up on Legs' right side, she turned to greet him, and I got a hint of her side profile. But it was still hard to see from where I sat. She had no bangs, not like Laurie, just a sidewall of hair coming to below her chin. I could just make out the tip of a tiny nose poking out. I figured that nose could have had a ring in it. That seemed right.

I found myself wishing that I knew what was on that napkin in Ralphie's hand. I'd find out soon enough, soon as Ralphie came back looking dejected and let me in on it. But a part of me wished I knew before he presented it to her. So I could hope on it. So I could put a silent prayer on the words there. Part of me wanted that knowledge purged from my mama's books to work for him.

Ralphie laid that napkin note on the bar, to the side of Legs, and gingerly pushed it in front of her. The note disappeared from my sightline. She turned back to the bar. Her body was still. Her head stayed looking down and slightly cocked. Then her face turned back to look up at Ralphie, standing barrel-chest-big-bearded next to her. I'd never seen Ralphie so confident in the presence of a woman before.

Legs reached her hand right out and placed it on his hairy forearm. Ralphie smiled, and looked like he was going to say something, or maybe even cry a little.

I'm not sure if he got a word (or a tear) out.

About this time, there was a splintering sound as the front door to the bar was kicked open and Ralphie's Uncle Timmy walked in. And instead of all of us looking at Legs and Ralphie, now we were all looking at Uncle Timmy—a 12-gauge in his hands, a roll of duct tape worn over each of his wrists like a superhero's iron bracelets.

"Ev'rybody on the gud'damn ground!" he shouted.

"Whoooo-Hooooo!" Woo-Hoo yelled as Tricia ducked below the bar to get out of firing range.

"Ev'rybody but Woo-Hoo get the fuck down," Uncle Timmy said, correcting himself. "He's given his service for this country. He can stay sittin'."

"Uncle Timmy?" Ralphie said from his position next to Legs. He was probably thinking the same thing I was thinking: *Duct tape bracelets?*

"You're not a part of this, Ralphie, and you're not a vet," Uncle Timmy said, "so you're gonna have to get down now." He gestured to the floor with the barrel of the 12-gauge.

"But, I wrote a note for this lady," Ralphie said, pointing to Legs.

"Well, that's down right sweet, nephew. And I'm sorry to interrupt. But something tells me this lady has another agenda. Lacey?" Timmy said nodding at the woman next to Ralphie.

The woman he called "Lacey" brought Ralphie's note napkin to her lips and deposited a kiss on it. She took the note and shoved it into Ralphie's front jeans' pocket, her fingers lingering there a minute by the tiny bronze nipple rivet. She whispered something into his ear. Then she helped Ralphie to the ground and onto his stomach, and he let his belly go slack again.

Then Uncle Timmy and Lacey used those duct tape bracelets to congeal our wrists and ankles together ('cept Woo-Hoo, that is), and took our wallets, and one of the burnouts tried to complain and got his mouth taped.

Timmy took the register's cash and promised everyone present it was nothing personal.

Lacey and Timmy kissed quickly on the lips, like they were in a movie, and then left. The front door swung shut behind them. Woo-Hoo was still sitting at the bar taking sips of his Pabst, looking like he was about ready for another. His eyes never left Trish down there on the floor behind the bar. The burnout with the taped mouth was sobbing some in the corner.

Ralphie and I lay there, hogtied and duct taped on our bellies, for a while. We looked at each other. The bar's floor smelled like fresh dirt, and old dish towels, and older rot. But Ralphie's baby face, under his Black Forest beard, was smiling from ear to ear. I imagine he was still thinking about that kiss he got, that napkin crumpled into his front pocket, and how close Lacey's hands had gotten to his man parts. I arched my back and shook my head trying to figure what the chances of all this transpiring the way it had was.

We all stayed quiet for a bit. I silently wished the best for Timmy and Legs. I wondered then if I'd ever meet a woman like that, the kind of person you'd rob other people for. That's a special one.

I asked Ralphie later about that napkin, but he never did tell me what was written on it, just carried it around in his wallet like a lucky amulet or something.

The law ended up catching Lacey and Uncle Timmy not too far out of town that same night. They'd pulled over on the shoulder for a celebratory copulation and had seen the red and blue lights too late. When I saw Lacey's picture in the paper the next day, it turned out she wasn't as pretty as I thought she'd be.

Ralphie and I kept working in the woods and going to Gruff's afterwards. And I started falling asleep everywhere. I started getting out of bed less and losing more of my damned eyelashes.

Ralphie kept getting updated reading lists from Timmy, back in prison again. Turns out, Timmy *was* quite the avid reader once you took away his 12-gauge.

One day I got a letter from Laurie that said she missed me. Said she could use some money. Said she was pregnant and it might be mine. I'm not much good at gestational math, but I was pretty sure that was impossible. But I did still miss her. And all the same, I figured maybe I could hand-deliver that money and see how she was. Maybe stay out there a bit. Nothing I was dead set on yet, just thinking, maybe. If that little 'un didn't have a daddy and all...well everybody could use one.

While I loaded the last of my things into the Ford, Ralphie said he was proud of my "chivalrous ways" (big words for Ralphie, but he *had* been reading more). He slapped my shoulder and asked, "When did you start reading your mama's books, you romantic, you?"

"Don't wait up," I told him, and smiled and nodded. I was going to miss Ralphie if everything worked out with Laurie and me.

I blinked down at the steering wheel of my '82 Ford Ranger. The woven interior smelled like old gasoline and fresh wood. The bed rattled around at any speed over thirty, even with my stuff back there weighing it down.

I didn't lose any lashes the whole trip out to see Laurie. When I got there, I didn't feel like sleeping for two whole days. We just kept talking, her and me.

And when that baby was finally born, he didn't look a lick like me, and that's probably just as well. I've never been the handsomest man. But Laurie wanted to call him Sammy Jr. anyway—"After you," she said.

I suggested the middle name be Davis, but she wouldn't go for it.

"What? Sammy Davis Jr.," I said.

She said it'd be too confusing with the kid not being black or Jewish or anything. And she played it so straight-faced it made me laugh off and on for hours.

That night I proposed to her on a decorative napkin.

I told Ralphie about it.

Now Sammy Jr.'s old enough to start laughing for himself. And that laugh sounds just like a tiny me, minus the whiskey, minus the cigarettes, minus the miles. I still can't figure out how it is Jr. sounds so much like me. Maybe I'm just thinking it, projecting it or something. I think about all kinds of nonsense while watching Jr. sleep. Sometimes I fall asleep with him, but I can't sleep like he can. I'm just not that tired anymore.

The Road to Thebes

The first time I remember seeing my dad, I'm 33. He's a foot shorter than me. He has freckles, like our family dog. He has an accent half Dominican, half Harlem, half something else; a smile I don't trust. He's a carnival mirror I can't stop looking for myself in. It's the way he scans his environment, like me. The way he smiles at everybody but puts the serious on quick. The way he's trying to play off this meeting on the ground floor entrance of his apartment complex as happenstance, like Uncle Cecil hadn't warned him with a covert phone call on the subway ride over. Dad's words express surprise. But Dad's eyes are my eyes. And I can see right through him.

The thing is, even though this guy's such a shitty actor, a part of me still wants to believe in him.

When he says, "Oh my God, are jou mine?" and pulls my sister, Laura, and me in and says, "Jou're beautiful," he sounds so sincere. And that catches me off-guard.

He tells us to call him "Papi" like they do in the D.R. "Papi" pronounced 'poppy' like the plant they make heroin from.

Papi and Laura and I are standing between these two sets of glass doors with our arms around each other, our necks bent inward, our heads together as one. And it feels, almost, euphoric.

Uncle Cecil, who brought us here, begs off quickly, saying he doesn't get along with Papi's girl. Laura thanks Cecil, gives him a hug, and he's out. Papi nods to a security guard sitting in a booth behind a thick sheet of glass. The security guard nods, presses a button for the inner set of glass doors to open. We walk inside. Papi presses the up arrow for the elevator.

When we enter Papi's apartment, on the seventh floor, his girl's in the kitchen wearing a floral scarf around her head. She says she's a cancer survivor. It's the first thing she says.

The second thing she says is, "Jou here for money or somethink?" and isn't joking, but tries to act like she is.

Papi starts talking, and it's like he's trying to paddle against two opposing currents of a river; one current his past, one current his present. But he keeps smiling to make it seem effortless. He's a strong swimmer. We all eat the chicken his girl cooks. It's tender and perfectly spiced with cumin and chili.

There's this point where we're all sitting in the living room and Laura asks Papi why he hit our mom when they were together, when I was a baby, before she was born. And he says, "I didn't. Lorda, I didn't."

And she says, "Yes, you did. My mom wouldn't lie."

And Papi says, "Okay. I made a mistake. I made a mistake, Lorda."

And she's the parent and he's the kid begging for forgiveness and I just don't want to be here.

At the end of the night, Papi walks us to the subway. The crook of his arm is linked in the crook of Laura's arm. He says how much he loves us. He says we'll meet up in the morning.

On the train ride back to our Bronx hotel, I tell Laura, "That guy's full of shit."

The next day Papi isn't returning Laura's calls. She keeps calling him.

I tell her to forget it, to forget him. I say, "Fuck that guy."

But eventually he answers and asks us if we can meet him at the edge of Manhattan.

On the subway ride in, Laura asks me to give Papi a chance. She says, "This shit has to be weird for him, too."

She's right. She's always been more forgiving than me.

When we arrive at the designated location, I'm surprised that Papi's there. The three of us nod and hug and board another train to our aunt's apartment in Queens.

"I remember when jou was a baby," our aunt tells me while we sit at her kitchen table. That's the last time she'd seen me. I don't remember it, but she does.

She has a picture she took of my mom and Papi holding me up between them on their wedding day. But Papi's sister has never seen my sister; she doesn't have a picture of her. There's no question whose she is, though. My mom was pregnant with Laura when she left our dad. Laura looks just like me, just like Papi. Papi and her are the same height.

The whole time we're at our aunt's, Papi's phone keeps blowing up in his pocket. He ignores it. A couple of times he looks at the screen and blows it off.

My phone starts ringing, but I don't recognize the number.

"Who is it?" Papi asks.

"I don't know," I say.

"Let me see," he says. "Oh, jou gotta answer it, Papito. Tell her I'm not wit jou."

"I'm not really comfortable with that, man," I say. "I'll just let it ring."

"Hason," he says. "Jou my son, I'm asking this one thing. Can jou help me?"

Papi doesn't know me, so he doesn't know I hate lying, even to people I don't like. But, somehow, despite this, I still do what he asks. I answer my phone the next time it rings and tell his girl, "Naw, I don't know where Ramon is."

"I know he's with jou, Hason!" she yells. "Don't jou fuckink lie to me!"

"Sorry," I say, "I'll tell him to call you if I see him."

She starts in again and I hang up on her.

"What did she say?" Papi asks.

"She's convinced you're with us, man. You better come up with a good alibi."

I feel like Papi's mistress.

"Thank jou, Hason," he says. "I know jou didn't want to, but jou did that for me? Thank jou."

I keep getting little glimpses of why my sister is always looking for *this* guy; for *this* kind of confirmation. Papi puts one hand on my shoulder and squeezes, and I don't show it, but inside I'm fucking melting like some newly-found orphan being given a puppy.

"Hey, you're my Papi," I say. And I get a taste of what having a proud father might be like. And now, Papi and me, we have this between us. Even if it's only this little, sticky bond of deceit, it's more than we had. It's a pact we can share. Something we can build on.

We leave our aunt's, promising to call, and the three of us walk back to the subway. Papi and Laura have their arms linked again. His phone's still ringing, but it's just background noise; it's been ringing about every five minutes, all day. Maybe he doesn't know how to silence it.

Just before we reach the subway Papi pulls his phone out and says, "Ello?" He speaks fast Spanglish. Then low and slow. Then he hangs up and stares at the station platform.

"What's up, Papi?" I ask.

"Oh, jou know, she's angry," he says rolling his eyes.

"What'd you tell her?"

"I had to tell her I was with jou and jour sister."

There's this ball of heat that starts thick in my chest and goes straight through the top of my head.

"You threw me under the bus?" I say. "What the fuck's wrong with you?"

I look at Laura and see the fear on her face; like I might fuck this up, like I might forever exile *this* guy from our future. She's the only reason I turn and walk to the edge of the platform and stare down at the tracks. There's a bunch of trash down there, old wrappers and shit. I find myself looking for the third rail, for the widow-maker they're always talking about in East Coast rap songs.

I hear Papi say, "Lorda, talk to jour bruda," like I'm some sulking kid, and it's all I can do to not turn around and beat the last thirty-three years out of *this* fucking guy.

Laura walks to my side and stares at the tracks with me.

"You...all right?" she asks.

I stare until the rails go blurry and the trash down there disappears.

I don't cry easily. And I don't cry now.

Instead I say, "I swear to God, Lu, if he comes over here...I'm throwing his ass in front of the next train." I say the last part loud enough for Papi to hear.

Laura nods. She knows me. She knows I haven't been in a fight since I was a teenager, but that right now I'm so fucking angry, that this part of me has always been angry. That I just need space. I need time.

"I just need a minute," I say.

She nods and walks back to where Papi sits. She stands at his side, looking down at him.

I hear her ask him one word. "Why?"

And the way her voice shakes, it makes me want to hurt Papi more.

I hear him trying to console her with that Dominican smoothness. That: *Lorda, Lorda.* I picture him trying to talk his way out of shit with my mom, in that same voice. I wonder why I ever let my guard down around this dude.

I think of how the world's so fucking backwards. How we're born with open arms and slowly learn to close them in around ourselves to keep everything else out. How on the subway ride back into the city I stumble as the train stops short and Papi cowers, like I'm going to hit him. How I feel like an abusive son because of this. How I hate him, but I still end up hugging him when he opens his arms before disappearing again. How I know I'll never see or hear from him after this.

How I never do.

How I feel like I should be okay with that.

And I am. And I'm not.

And I don't know what that says about me.

The Case for Viable Life in Atlantis

<u>Opening Argument</u> – The surf

Picture it. The sun is 92.9 million miles away, but it is still present on your skin; as present as the sand and wind and surf and salt in the air. Can you taste it? Time and space are falling asleep on large beach blankets purchased from small kiosks and waking up groggy alongside you. A breeze is blowing. Giant leaves of the palm trees sway on the jetty in the distance. Earth's age is somewhere between midday and sunset.

From out of the waves a brunette mermaid is ambling, slithering—bare-breasted and dripping—clutching a burlap sack in her fist. The sack is full. She's using it as a makeshift cane. She stops in front of you and begins pulling objects out—a pie-shaped broken clay shard, a rusty jungle gym bar, Poseidon's decapitated head still grinning.

The mermaid is placing each relic beneath a promise in the wet sand, covering and rearranging them, asking you to point to the Queen of Spades within this Three Card Monty. But there are no cards. There is no Queen. And if you become too focused on a Queen, you begin to disregard the truths she's revealing. If you question too deeply whether mermaids are real or not, you start to lose the meaning of everything else. If you're not careful, you'll start falling back to sleep on your blanket. The palm trees in the distance.

And what if you did fall asleep? And awoke, not on your blanket, but underwater? How long do you suppose you could hold your breath?

That's the real question. That's why we're here today.

How long?

I'll bet it's longer than you think.

Exhibit A – The bottle

The ship leans drastically portside, and Robin (the cabin boy), and Theodore (the deck hand), and Samuel (the Captain) slide across the top deck and over the railing out into the sea. The ocean doesn't smile or laugh or care, it just digests what it's given, the same way it's polished every rough edge smooth since the beginning of the beginning of the before. The same way it sent man forth, from coral embryonic birthing sacs, into the open air without clothing. The way mans' tears in the Midwest still taste like salt on sandy lips and hot faces.

Tommy (the stowaway)'s hair falls out of his cap, and he is revealed not to be a boy at all but a downplayed young woman with bound breasts and charcoal cheeks. The ship veers further off course, further portside; its remaining sail is only partially attached, blowing like a white flag in the darkness. Tommy loses her footing and spills over the deck into the ocean. The ship disappears behind her into darkness. Others spill over after Tommy. Robin is among them.

The sea's stubbornness, and the inherent voodoo of the tropics, brings Robin (the cabin boy) and Tommy (our charcoal cheeked stowaway) together again upon a deserted island in the Atlantic. They wash up on separate pieces of the same bow. They stare in disbelief at the sand upon their knees until daylight.

The day passes. They find fish. They find shelter. They find shells.

The next night they begin naming the stars above them, one each night, as they come into existence; one star named for every shipmate that washes up facedown, for the next five days.

The first stars are called *Rod-235D*, *Terran Casper-4H*, and *Heron-12*.

On the sixth night, after the bodies have stopped coming in, Robin points to a cluster of stars that looks like a three-headed dog and says, "*Precious-1*," and kisses Tommy on her cheek.

"*Faithium North*," Robin dubs a cluster that looks like a baby holding a trident.

"*Reasonia Left*," Tommy calls three lonely stars that aren't always there.

"*Lovene FN*," Robin says pointing to an atomic ball of twine getting bigger with every passing night.

But none of the stars know their own names. None of the constellations have any idea they exist. Robin and Tommy are never found. Nobody would have ever known they were here had their bottled message not washed up on the South Carolina coastline a hundred years later.

Exhibit B – Memory

If I could direct your attention to the boy in the back row of the choir. The boy with the Clark Kent cowlick accenting his forehead, his hands clasped somewhere behind him, his eyes staring out over an ocean of attendees looking for their offspring on the stage.

The boy in question is at the top of his game—not only in reference to his placement on the podium (he is clearly an up-and-coming crooner), but he also wears a large-sized varsity jacket in the halls between classes and is a local ballet attendee. Yes, a local ballet attendee. He is not ashamed of the gravitational pulls he feels toward things that may or may not *go together*. He looks you in the eye when he considers sentence formation. He speaks like a firm handshake, adjusting its grip accordingly.

Every Tuesday and Thursday between the hours of three and five p.m., the boy volunteers at the hospice center because he believes that wisdom is contagious and he wishes to catch it.

At the hospice center, he asks Margaret, and George, and Adam (all dying of old age) the same question:

"*What do you remember of your first love?*"

And Margaret, and George, and Adam all say the same thing, at different times: "I can picture [him/her] like it was yesterday.

But I can't, for the life of me, tell you what I had for breakfast this morning."

The boy wonders if memory is a blessing or a fluke or a bit of both depending on what we ask of it.

"Thank you for coming, Herman," says Margaret at the end of the boy's visit. Margaret is the only one who gets the boy's name right.

"Thank you for asking, Horace," says George smiling, his eyes squinting. George has hyponatremia. The boy puts a pinch of salt in George's water glass every visit.

"Thank you for being here, Seahorse," says Adam. Adam's Alzheimer's is affecting his hippocampus.

The hippocampus of the human brain looks strikingly like a seahorse, hence its name. *Hippos*: meaning horse. *Kampos*: meaning sea monster.

Exhibit C – The bathtub acoustics

One day, Alfonse Tibbett walked out into the surf off the New Hampshire coast. Alfonse walked seaward until his pants and shirt were completely drenched and clinging to his body. Soon the ocean waters immersed his chest. The waves crested against his face. The salt stuck thick to the tight curls in his hair. He spat out the frothing sea and continued to walk east, toward the horizon, until his head went under the water and he disappeared.

Abraham Shelton (a man, just a man, only a man) saw Alfonse walking into the ocean. He attempted to reach Alfonse but could not salvage him. Abraham retreated from the water to the beach, defeated. With his clothes dripping, he began yelling for help.

The Coast Guard could also not find Alfonse, despite its helicoptering efforts. Everyone assumed the waters had had their way with him.

A year later, a man (with a strikingly similar description to Alfonse) walks from the waves onto the same beach that Alfonse had disappeared on. The man is naked save strands of algae clinging to the bony prominences at his shoulders and waist. He spits out a mouthful of seawater at the feet of a Mr. and Mrs. William Aikens, and says, "Atlantis is a beautiful place to visit, but..." then shrugs his shoulders and walks west, carrying what Mrs. Aikens calls a *mermaid's purse*—which is not an actual purse but a shark egg casing (this may, or may not, be important). She notices the neck of a bottle sticking out of the shark egg.

A naked man (again, fitting Alfonse's physicality) is spotted multiple times in the Appalachian Mountains. Overnight hikers claim to hear what they collectively describe as: *"A man singing to the night in an unknown language."* Some suggest it's just an emaciated, intoxicated, over-elated moonshiner.

One local resident stated, "If you've ever put yer head underwater in the bathtub, and listened to yerself breathin', the singin' kinda sounds like that. It's a slippery whisper."

I ask you to try and recollect the sound from inside your bathtub, in your head, right now.

Exhibit D – The reflex

Allow me to get personal for a moment.

When I was an infant, my father threw me in a lake. It's what his father did to him, and what my father's grandfather put his son through. We don't have daughters. I don't know why that is. With each generation, it is a different lake the son is tossed in. With each generation, we come closer to something beyond us.

I don't remember this particular event because I was too young, but I know the story. I'm sure my father remembers it, but he doesn't talk about it. My oldest brother tells it best. He says that only a couple of seconds after my head went underwater, my father jumped in. This was the first time he'd initiated me in a lake. I must have been a month old, maybe less.

My father was wearing some of those tiny, tight swim trunks all fathers of that time wore. My brother says it felt like father was down there, in the lake, in those tight trunks, for a long time before resurfacing. My mother says that all her other babies floated, but I didn't.

"That's why he dove in," she says, "because you sank like a ball of lead."

When my father came up for the first time he said, "I can't find him."

He was trying to hide his panic. He blew his nose and went back under.

When my father came up the second time he said, "His legs are stuck in something."

This is the point where my mother started crying.

My brother was torn between jumping into the lake with my father and making sure there were no makeshift weapons for my mother to kill my father with if he resurfaced without me.

On the third dive, my brother accompanied him. When my father came up for the fifth time he had me in one hand; a twisted, broken branch in the other. My brother says that I was not breathing. He says our father put me on the shore and started blowing into my mouth. He says that on the third breath I opened my eyes and just stared up at them.

My father stared down. I didn't spit up any water. I just looked at him.

My mother cried, "Oh, thank goodness!"

And only then did I start crying. I haven't cried since.

All of my family members there that day swear that I was underwater for far too long. You may say that their fear affected their perception of time. And I would agree, but you should know that my father was an experienced diver; he could hold his breath for many minutes on end. So it's quite possible that I *was* down there for an extended period of time. Maybe I was in some kind of air pocket. Maybe I only nearly drowned and my father revived me. Maybe my mammalian diving reflex was activated—this happens to children under a certain age—and the reflex sent me into a type of instant hibernation that suppressed my body's need for oxygen. Say what you want, but I'm here; alive and breathing, so...

The prosecution will, no doubt, ask that you judge all the evidence in front of you—and all that I have yet to present—from a buoyant position relative to your Body Mass Index. He will say these are all just unrelated stories, ridiculous antidotes. And *maybe* they are.

But what I'm asking is that you let your life vests float away for an evening. Don't worry about what you'll have for lunch tomorrow. Don't worry about how much salt you'll put on it. Close your eyes and focus on breathing differently. Focus on the hippocampus, the seahorse of the head. Focus on the human body being 60 percent water; have faith in that. Put your head back in the bathtub tonight and listen for what you can't seem to remember. Think about where we started, long ago; with no God, no lips, no legs, no language.

Breathe differently.

Maybe nothing on this earth can drown you.

Maybe you still have gills and have just forgotten how to use them.

When we reconvene tomorrow, I ask that you come back open-minded.

Closing Statement – The glass box

In the middle of the courtroom is your classic magician's water tank, big enough for a man. It is three feet by three feet by seven feet tall. The glass is three inches thick. It is framed in welded steel. As you can see the box is filled with water. Don't worry. There will be no curtains or illustrious assistant. This isn't a trick. I'm not an illusionist. I'm a person, a mere person, on the precipice of the truth. I'm hoping you are also that kind of person.

As we well know, the truth is elusive. It requires a kind of sight most don't have. Everything has not "*come to this;*" this is just where we are. This is not *fate*. This is not *faith*-based. Those are both concepts. This tank and its water have substance. The evidence I am about to present is as solid as a lump of lead sinking in a lake. Yes, that is a bottle submerged in the tank. Yes, it is the same bottle that once contained a note with the name of the star *Faithium North*. *Faithium North*, an actual place, not a religion.

As you can see, I have my son with me. He is eight-months-old. His name is Will. Will knows the lake waters well, all waters well. I have been introducing him to them since his birth. He was even born underwater, in a lake not far from here. And I'll let you know his mother, God bless her soul, would want this if she were still here. She prepared him for this, in her own way, as I am preparing you.

The water tank before you is for Will. Will is going to show us what humanity is capable of. He is going to help us remember the truths we've forgotten, the truth you are going to be witness to today. Do not worry that Will's cry sounds different; he has been in the open air for much longer than normal. Too long, almost. Trust me, crying is just the way he expels the build-up of air from his lungs. Yes, he sounds different. Don't worry, he's okay. Focus on the water. Focus on the bottle.

Do not be afraid when his lips begin turning blue after his submersion in the tank. Blue is good for him. It's the new you. It's the new me. This is all part of the great process of us. Fear is the only thing holding us back from being like Will.

Oh, thank you for the hand, Bailiff.

I am now going to put Will into the—

Bailiff, what are you doing?

Bailiff, take your hands off me!

Judge?

Bailiff, take your hands off my son! Put him down. Put him in the water!

NO! I will not have *the right*, sir! I will not *be silent*! Your Honor? Bailiff, let go of me. Your Honor, I am not finished. The defense does *not* rest.

Jurors, the truth requires a token. You have to trust that I would never hurt my son. Jurors, take off your precious mental life vests and put my son in the glass box. If only for a few minutes. Please, he requires it! Listen to how his cries are changing.

Bailiff, if you give me a minute you'll see that my son is not like you. He is beyond us. He is—if you would just put him in the water!

Your Honor, the defense does not rest!

The defense does not rest!

The defense does not...

Inventorying the
Future's Armory

7.

Over Sierra's shoulder, a maybe-five-year-old girl is shooting her father in the face. The gun looks real, but it can't be, she's giggling so sweetly. She must be pantomiming the recoil, her elbows kicking back in sudden blasts of imagination. Blast. Pause. Blast. Pause. Her could-be father is taking each invisible bullet. His mouth contorting into Billy Idol lips—one side raised and the other side slightly melted. He's surrendering to gravity pretended. He wobbles unsteadily, falls to his knees, rolls back onto the grass. The daughter stands to his side, reloads the silver revolver, fires again. She tucks the gun into the sash of her white-trimmed dress. Lies down next to the could-be father. Holds his hand. There are seven invisible bullets left inside him.

6.

Beyond the five-year-old girl and her could-be-father, a boy rides an old Schwinn toward the Wheel of Ferris. Electric lights illuminate from the center and disappear into the air surrounding the carnival basecamp. Red and blue triangle-flags flap from white ribbon. The boy's mother once told him, "With every turn of the crank you spin the world beneath you." He presses the left pedal of the Schwinn and a piece of the road disappears under him. He presses the right pedal and the Wheel of Ferris digs at Earth in the distance. His father's machete lays sheathed and swathed on the boy's back. Before, his father would have hacked trails in the tall grass behind their house with the machete, but now his father is grinding teeth somewhere far east. His father doesn't have an old bicycle to spin Earth with. He will have bodies to plant and hearts to win. The boy will have hearts to win, too. And large stuffies with animal faces to gift. He hopes. If he wins. He wonders if Ruth Ann will be at the carnival in her white trimmed dress. His leg comes up, and the pocket knife presses against his thigh. The Y top of a slingshot waves a slow goodbye from his back pocket. He wonders why he has so many weapons on him. Right pedal. Left pedal. There are six bicycle crank rotations before the carnival will reach him.

5.

I look away from the Wheel of Ferris. And the boy. And the five-year-old girl and her father. Sierra lowers her forehead, in front of me, and looks up. Her eyes are bigger like this. I can see myself falling asleep among the flecks of her hazel irises. I pull my eyes away. There's a strain in my neck. I can feel Sierra still looking up at me. The smell of something dangerously delicious is cooking somewhere. Clouds are bunching overhead. At the carnival, a hot air balloon is anchored to the ground by an elephant chained to a giant wooden stake. There are five seconds left on an oven timer threatening to ding, ding, ding.

4.

Foremost, our forefathers founded forts in the East that expanded outward, across the Great Plains and fortified mountain ranges; left the smell of foregone feathers falling; the promise of forward progression becoming a mantra exhaled in great gasps of fossil fuels. The future consists of numbers counting backwards. The forecast is calling and hanging up when we answer. The clouds are clumping overhead by the bushel. A forefinger and a thumb are pinching off the heads of unborn relatives between now and forever.

3.

The clouds part for a second, like dance instructors morphing from individual trees, into a collective donut. The center of the donut jellies and swirls. The little girl in the grass is sitting up, double checking the revolver's cylinder for bullets. The carnival has adopted another elephant to hypnotize fairgoers into the big tent. The carnival is becoming a circus. Everything a circus. Three rings. High rent. The boy's father is knee deep in muddy innards, on another continent, and associating the ooziness surrounding him with blood pudding, and having waking dreams of never eating again. My pulse is beating like a drum in the Circle of Willis—the Ferris of the head. The third cranial nerve is controlling the movement of my eyes, the tenth the quickening of my heart, the seventh my taste (for significance). I wish I knew more about the displacement of nitrogen and the ascension rate formulas for rising quickly from warm waters into uncertain environments. I wish I had an oxygen chamber for the delirium to come; more couches to crash on; more friends with basements. Wish I could live in the dark dankness of the undergrowth, becoming the overhead plumbing, and the illusion of being the secret lying beneath it all. But I'm above ground and impatient. There are three reasons to keep your respiratory rate regulated if you believe in them.

2.

It takes two to make a thing. It takes blood, and subatomic dust, and seamen adapted to naval conditions to bring life into a surfactant bundled, pre-wrapped blanket. It takes the second wave of the attack to land the boy's father close enough to the beach of some god-awful continent. His father's feet don't know the difference between the submerged turtle's backs and his friend's sinking helmets. His feet only know the feel of their position in the shifting sands. The hard shells. It would be nice if it was all turtles down there on the ocean floor, but that would only be more Eastern mystic bullshit mixed with sentiment and sediment and oil. What if it was helmets all the way down; a world balanced on infinite packs of Lucky Strikes, and nudie pics, and spent bullets, and chaw spit? A terrible and comforting vision. And his boy knows nothing of this, as he reaches the carnival grounds, on his blue Schwinn, and is asked to join the circus. "We will be leaving soon," says The Man With The Top Hat. And the boy on the Schwinn says he never leaves where he's at. And The Strong Man with the moustache laughs at the concept of pedaling the world to you, but The Fat Lady With The Beard nods and tilts her head at the boy's magic. The could-be father is looking for imaginary bullet casings in the grass. His daughter begins to doubt whether her real-deal father would ever pretend to search for anything he couldn't already see, and the bullets are solidifying, and becoming real, inside the no-longer-father's chest and head. He falls down again, with less theatrics. The real, and the surreal, and the unreal are taking turns crouching and leapfrogging over each other. Just turn on your TV set. There is a father on the wrong part of the planet, and a father in the vanity strip between the asphalt and the pavement. Sierra and I are staring at each other, under a funnel cloud, two seconds before impact.

1.

The first thing to consider is that the letter "I" is a pronoun and number. Math is a constant. The future deals in constants. It counts backwards. Its native tongue is Subtraction. The five-year-old daughter is every age and always five years old again. Her could-be father, is no-longer-a father, and every man she sees him in. The boy on the Schwinn joins the circus and brings the world to him, but his father comes back from the world different. His father comes back bearing too many helmets. The storm clouds above Sierra and me are the ghosts I thought I was, and the ghosts I haven't become yet. They are sure friends. Sierra is pulling on the drawstrings of my hoodie trying to calm me, trying to crawl into me, trying to save us from the nature of our existence. I tell her that years after the boy joins the circus; the five-year-old girl comes to his Baseball Toss stand and knocks down the milk bottle pyramid. "Nobody ever wins this," he says. "But I won," she says. "I won it." And the boy nods and gives the girl his sheathed machete and slingshot. He keeps his pocket knife for peeling apples later. He shows her where she can find a Schwinn, and teaches her the secrets of pedaling it. She gives him the silver revolver and a handful of bullets and a kiss on the cheek. The boy says, "Thank you, Ruth Ann."

"What happens next?" asks Sierra.

I tell her that the girl pedals into the hills. I tell her she finds family there.

"I, one," Sierra says. The pronoun and the number. Her eyes close.

I bend down as she rises. Our lips touch. My lips cultivating a taste for her Chapstick—cranial nerve seven—Strawberry Fade Fanatic.

Sierra pulls back from our first kiss having not been struck by lightning, having not been pulled into the eye of a great whirlwind, having not had her heart melt out of her chest and solidify in my hands.

"We might not be right for this," Sierra says. "You seem pretty distracted."

I don't tell her that she's the distraction. Don't say how the future counts in reverse and assigns each of us a weapon but never trains us how to use it. How addition is a risk but subtraction is a promise.

I just nod and squint at the explosions behind her.

She turns to look where I'm looking. Toward the pillars of light. The clouds forming from the ground and spreading across an invisible ceiling. The end of the beginning. And the beginning of the beginning. And, the end.

"I think," she says, "I hear my mother calling."

Closer

Lionel wondered when exactly he had started positioning himself closer to people, to strangers, on purpose. On the city bus, he would feel letdown if there was an open double-seat waiting for him because he'd have to take it, out of social expectations, and then he wouldn't be sitting next to anyone. He started riding the bus only during rush hour. Even if he had no place to be. Just to be forced to sit closely.

This was why Lionel started viewing films again in the theaters. He and Ethel would go when they were younger, but then she stopped wanting to go out, and then she grew sick and sicker.

He picked opening nights to see new films. And if the foot or leg or hand of a person sitting next to him accidentally grazed his, he would remain frozen in the exact position, hoping it would happen again—the hairs on his hand or leg or arm (whichever had been grazed) left standing at attention. He felt the proximity of each individual hair—the electricity there. He found himself paying closer attention to the space between him and everyone.

When Lionel wasn't riding buses or in crowded theaters (or at home alone with the ceramic angel collection that Ethel had loved so much, the kissing angels especially), he found small cafes or shared-table sushi restaurants or waiting rooms in county-run facilities to occupy. Whether he had an appointment at the facility or not, he would walk into the lobby and sit down. He liked listening to the turning of pages, the hushed conversations. When he did have an appointment, he liked the dentist's chair. He liked the hygienist's shoulder or arm or breast grazing his head. Not that the breast was any better than the shoulder or the arm. It really wasn't. It wasn't a sickness. *He* wasn't sick. If anything, he was only lonely. And there was nothing morally wrong with loneliness. He considered putting an ad out for a roommate but wasn't convinced he should. He didn't know if he'd like *that*. There might be undesired dialogue involved. Lionel was much more of a conversational voyeur. He liked to listen, not participate. The only person he still enjoyed conversation with was Ethel, at the cemetery on Holgate. And there, Ethel was always the voyeur. She couldn't help but be.

It wasn't until Lionel found himself using the middle of three urinals, in the bathroom of a downtown bookstore, that he wondered if he hadn't purposely put himself in this compromising position.

When Lionel had first entered the restroom all the urinals had been unoccupied, the entire bathroom had been unoccupied, and he'd told himself that he just *happened* to walk to the middle urinal—that his actions were absent-minded. But Lionel had known, and practiced, correct urinal etiquette for his entire life. He deeply understood that you should try to put as much porcelain and hanging metal half-walls between piss streams as possible. He hadn't done that this time.

Sitting next to someone on the bus or in the theater was one thing, it was innocent, but pissing next to them was certainly another.

If someone walked in, with him peeing in the middle urinal, and wanted to pee as well (without having to aim into a toilet) that person would be forced to piss in one of the urinals directly on either side of him.

Lionel told himself that the giant bookstore wasn't very busy, that he'd be okay. But what if someone did come in? He couldn't just *wrap it up* all quick and nifty like the prostate of his younger years. What if they thought he was the kind of person who wanted to turn his head and speak directly into their ear, or glance down to see what they were "working with," or comment on the quality of the stream they were producing?

When Lionel was a child, his father had been a voracious bathroom commentator and Lionel had hated him for it. It was one of the reasons Lionel always questioned whether he would be a suitable parent. How much of his father was in him?

"Look at you! You're pissing a rope, son!" his father would proudly proclaim to a restroom full of patrons at Fanny's Chicken

Shack, or the ball game, or whatever public bathroom they happened to be in together. And it was true—Lionel *had* pissed ropes back then, but he'd always known it was strange for his father to comment on it. He'd try to hold it until they got home, but he was never able to. His father would tell him that that was the curse of having a man's urethra coupled with the bladder of a Girl Scout.

A *Girl Scout*, he'd said that.

Lionel wondered if he shouldn't just scoot over to the next urinal—what his father would have called "switching lanes"—just in case somebody did come in from the bookstore. But he was already going, and it didn't seem worth it, or necessary, to pinch off and reposition now. Plus, he was pretty sure nobody really cared what old people did. Nobody cared what Ethel did toward the end. That she stopped smiling or making any sense. Only him.

Lionel was still staring at the wall in front of him, still thinking about *switching lanes*, when the bathroom door behind him opened and closed, and a bearded man—wearing a black t-shirt and green scarf—walked in. Lionel turned his head momentarily and gave a little nod, and immediately questioned this action. He didn't want to stand out. There were secret codes he didn't want to transmit. Maybe he shouldn't have done that. He'd never nodded to someone coming into a bathroom before.

The bearded man paused for a second, and then walked to the urinal to Lionel's right. The man smelled like mild sweat and sweet tobacco—like the thin cigars the neighbor kids smoked. The man had a wallet-chain jangling from his back pocket that connected to a belt loop at the front of his jeans. He bounced when he unzipped, and it sounded like a high school janitor laden heavy with keys echoing down the hallways. The man put his right hand on his hip and his left hand on the wall, creating a fleshy barrier between himself and Lionel with his upper arm. Lionel wondered if this was a defense mechanism—some kind of genius deterrent to prevent conversations in moments like this. It was a smart move.

The man wore brown work boots with the boot toes purposely worn away. There was dulling metal beneath the brown suede. Lionel guessed the man's feet were probably shoulder width apart. Lionel looked down at the black-and-white checkered tiles and his running shoes. They were comfortable, but stained. Maybe too comfortable. He'd need a new pair.

He looked confident, this man who stood with his shoulders leaned back and his hips pushed slightly forward. The first word that came to Lionel's mind was, *Regal*. It was a strange word to use to describe urinal technique, but it seemed fitting, here. More than fitting.

Regal.

Solid.

Regal.

Proper.

Suddenly, Lionel was positive that this was the way kings of the past had pissed—in an open, yet un-sloppy, stance. He wished *he'd* pissed that way more often as a young man. He wondered if he could start now, if it was too late for him to change everything.

And the quality of the bearded man's stream sounded thick. Hearty. Masculine. If Lionel had been a urinal talker, he would have had to comment on it. If this man had been his son, he'd be damned proud of him. And the sliver of water he glimpsed at the base of the man's urinal wasn't the least bit yellow. He probably made a good point to stay hydrated. Probably ate foods that were good for his prostate and plenty of greens. It seemed as if this man could piss, *would* piss, forever. There was no way that he got up multiple times a night to urinate. No way there were piss sprinkles left in his underwear after he'd tucked himself back in.

It wasn't until the man had stopped, and shook off, and zipped up, and turned to face Lionel that Lionel realized he probably shouldn't have been paying such close attention—realized he'd been kind of peeking between the man's arm and the metal divider for much too long.

Not that he was looking at anything in particular—he couldn't have seen *that* if he'd wanted to—he was just evaluating flow pressures from more than just an auditory standpoint, just appreciating this man's urethral vitality. And, that stance *was* powerful. But only Lionel's father would understand that kind of reasoning. And Lionel's father was strange by most standards and dead by years now. And suddenly he wasn't looking under the bearded man's arm but at the bearded man's chest and face and beard, his eyes continuing upward. He stopped as the man's thick eyebrows arched over his piercing, blue eyes.

And this wasn't a man, but a boy with a man's height and width and facial hair, and lead pipes for arms, and tattooed veins. He couldn't have been more than thirty, tops. A child really. He had hoop earrings in both of his earlobes. Not big hoops but small hoops.

What did that mean exactly?

Lionel couldn't remember.

Two small hoops? It was code for something that Lionel didn't understand.

And just as quickly as he'd taken this all in, Lionel shook his head back toward the wall in front of him, with his uncircumcised penis still in his hand, and this bearded stranger standing next to him. The man continuing to stare at him. Breathing on him. Lionel knew how guilty his turning away looked. An innocent man doesn't turn away like that, while using the middle urinal.

There was garlic on the young man's breath. His expirations felt heavy and measured and purposeful against Lionel's right ear and forehead. And Lionel wanted nothing more than to put his shriveled penis back in his pants. But he didn't, because he'd have to shake first. And a proper shaking was an endeavor at his age. He didn't want the man-boy to think he was finishing himself off or something. How many shakes were considered masturbation nowadays? What constituted a shake over a jiggle over a felony offense? What kind of message was he sending by looking, or not looking, at this man right now? Was it better to say something or remain silent? Didn't a senator play footsy with someone in the stall next to him once? How many earrings did that man have? Were they big or small? Whatever became of that?

Lionel refused to turn from the wall. His pride wouldn't allow it. He willed himself to pass through the wall and into wherever.

This wasn't like an unnoticed breast against his tufts of hair in the dentist's chair, or an accidental calf graze in the movie theater, this was uncharted and unwanted territory. He wished there was some way to go back in time and make the conscious decision to choose the urinal to the far left. He should have gone to the cemetery instead of the bookstore. He felt beads of sweat sprout all over his body. The man-boy standing next to him shook his head and blew one last, long, hot breath through his nostrils like some dragon on that HBO TV show that everybody couldn't get enough of lately. The dragon-man-boy hunched his shoulders before turning and slowly walking to the sink; his wallet-chain jangling at his side like a tiny broken shackle. Lionel heard the water running behind him, the gushing stream being broken by hands, the knob squealing shut. A paper towel dispensed and was torn and was crumpled. The metal lid of the garbage can slapped hard enough to keep it swinging on its hinge.

Lionel visibly jumped and screamed (a polytonal high-pitch scream, rising and falling quickly, becoming a whimpering, sputtering out) as he felt the splat and ooze of a wet and crumpled something hit and slop down the back of his head. Felt it slide off. Heard it splat on the linoleum.

He instantly felt stupid, knew that he hadn't been hurt, but only scared. Not scared, but humiliated by this bearded dragon-man-boy throwing a wetted paper towel at him. Still, just to make sure he wasn't hurt, Lionel reached his fingers back to where the balding was taking over. His hand felt wetness too cold to be blood. And this was his penance for using the middle of three urinals, for seeking seats next to people on buses, for wanting a hand to accidentally graze his in the theater, for going to the grave and telling Ethel all about it.

Lionel stood there, at the bookstore bathroom's middle urinal. Not turning. Wishing the towel had stuck to his head so he could focus on the point of pressure and not the spot of shame.

"What the fuck's wrong with you, old man?"

Lionel nodded to himself. He deserved it. He closed his eyes around it and waited for whatever was coming next.

Eventually the door to the bathroom slammed into the rubber grommet on the tile wall and squealed shut again.

Bathrooms are always tiled. Urinals are always porcelain. Grommets are always rubber.

110

It was a long time before Lionel stopped shaking. A longer time before he opened his eyes. But no matter how long he stood there, before zipping up, he knew there would be piss sprinkles in his underwear after tucking in.

And that's when he started to cry.

All the Same Ocean

My great-grandfather told my grandfather that when he turned eighteen he'd be on his own. This was by the Pacific coastline, somewhere in California. My grandfather grew up swimming in the waves and believing in a wisdom of observing a solid hour of digestion to avoid cramping. When he turned eighteen, he left home. He married a beautiful woman. He had a son, and a daughter (my mother), and another son. Together the five of them left the ocean for an orchard in Colorado. He gave up the waves for land. The edge for the middle. He cared for fruit trees in rows.

My grandfather told my mother and my two uncles the story of his leaving home at eighteen. When my mother graduated high school, she moved to New York City. When my Uncle Danny graduated, he joined her. They left the rows of trees for rows of buildings.

"I moved as far east as I could go without crossing an ocean," my mom was fond of saying.

In her Far East of America, Mom met a young man with a wide smile and dark skin and freckles. They walked through the rows of buildings together. The man was from the Dominican Republic—a half island south of there.

My mother always says, "I don't know how old your father really was when I met him."

She says, "He had good intentions but problems with the truth."

My father had other problems, too. Problems with women—as in, too many, too often. Problems with property and space perception—as in, an overabundance of stolen stereos in the living room of their apartment after the '77 blackout. He was too virile for his own good—as in, the birth of me in '78, the birth of my sister a year and a half later.

My parents were married in a small church when I was an infant. My mother wore a blue dress, my father a suit. I'm the chubby thing between them. They seem happy in the picture.

Less than a year later, my pregnant mother and I flew back to Colorado to put half a continent and orchards of trees between us and her husband (my father).

My sister was born.

My grandmother was sick for years.

My grandmother died. I wish I'd known her better.

My grandfather said her spirit went to heaven, while shielding his eyes so we wouldn't see his tears.

My sister kept looking for Grandma under the bed. She kept asking why Grandma was hiding.

I'm trying to find the rhythm between the downbeats and the upstrokes here. To see what jigsaw fragments fit into our family's folklore. We're horrible archivists. There is no overarching opus to point to and say, *"See that? That's where we come from."* Nothing to say, *"Because of that, this is where you're going."* We have dwindling numbers. We have a lack of traditions.

We say, "Time *ran away* with us."

We say, "I must have let that *slip through* the cracks."

I have a vague recollection of the way things happened.

My mother and sister and I moved from my grandfather's orchard to the next closest town: Grand Junction. Lu and I started elementary school and followed a giant irrigation ditch into the wilderness with a friend, and tried jumping our BMX bikes down half staircases every time we rewatched the movie *Rad*.

Mom got a good job with the city and started meeting less-than-desirable boyfriends who didn't trust the government.

Eventually, we moved from Colorado with one of those boyfriends and his giant dog, named Puppy, to Grayland—a town in Washington that doesn't really exist until you've been there and then becomes hazy again when you leave.

We stayed in a small single-story apartment by a clump of woods, covered in the mist banking off the ocean. I can only vaguely remember the town. It's fractured into three landmarks: the gas station, the Lamplighter Restaurant, and the sheriff's house (whose daughters all appeared to be Amazonians, the tallest and strongest girls I'd ever met). The ocean was only ten blocks from our front door through the woods and dunes.

I can remember floating with my sister on a giant piece of foam we found—four feet by four feet by one foot thick—out into the waves, trying to make it over the cresting white peaks and into the stillness of the sea.

"What were you thinking?" Mom said when she found out.

We weren't thinking. Not about our grandfather swimming in the Pacific. Not about our father crossing a portion of the Atlantic. Not about how it's all the same ocean that somebody schism-ed into different names to try to make sense of. As kids we were just on a piece of foam, hand-paddling toward the horizon.

I can still remember the way my skin itched like crazy under the warm shower water after being so cold for so long, after never successfully pushing past the high tide, after being beached again and again.

One day Mom's boyfriend and his giant dog, Puppy, decided to leave and not come back. Mom decided we'd move, in case he ever did. We packed a U-Haul and drove to Olympia.

In Olympia, one of my newfound friends chased me around our apartment flicking lit matches. One of the matches started a fire that burned inside my mattress. I tried to put it out. Tried to hide it, but it wouldn't stop smoking. When mom got home from work we put the internally burning bed outside.

This is not a metaphor.

I slept on the floor of my bedroom that night, missing the ocean of Grayland, while my mom and sister shared a bed in the room next to me. The next morning my mattress was a skeleton of scorched springs in the dumpster. The Australian band Midnight Oil had a popular song on the radio at the time, and after that night one of us would start singing the lyrics to the chorus,

"How can we dance when our earth is turning?"

And the rest of us would join in with,

"How do we sleep while our beds are burning?"

And then we'd laugh.

But I'd still feel a little pang of shame about it.

I'd think of our giant piece of foam in Grayland—how no matter how many times we were beached we still had that tangible, dirty, porous flotation device to try to reach the horizon. It felt familiar. It felt safe, even though it wasn't. It knew the ocean the way we did: as something giant and limitless, something to be feared and conquered, something to be moved by.

In the middle of the night, two months after moving to Olympia, my sister woke to see a flicker of light on the bedroom wall. She called my name and the light receded back down the hall, disappearing into the living room and slipping out the front door.

We discovered that that flickering light had left wax shapes on the carpet of our living room that could have been bad pentagrams or the erratic shakiness of an unsteady hand. It left wax drippings on mom's ID card but didn't take any money. It left us wondering if some past boyfriend had found us somehow.

While we were out the next day, somebody hammered in the dead bolt on our apartment door. Mom winced at the divots denting the wood. She covered the hole where the locking mechanism once was with her hand.

Again, not a metaphor.

That night we left the dishes in the sink.

We left no forwarding address.

We boarded a Greyhound bus south.

Two days later, we were on the doorstep of a women's shelter in Portland, Oregon, with a backpack apiece, smelling of Greyhound people and bus and station. In addition to my backpack, I had a faux leather zip-up briefcase in one hand—with every birthday card I'd ever received inside it—and a paper bag of plastic soccer trophies in the other.

At the women's shelter, we met a woman named Jude, who was born without eyes. It's called anophthalmia. Where Jude's eyes should have been there were two concave, smooth-skinned divots. She was always smiling. I liked watching how Jude listened.

Before long, the four of us moved into an apartment between Portland and Gresham. It was right on the MAX line, and *right* on the city line. The green sign that read "Welcome to Portland" was a half block to the west of us; the sign that read "Welcome to

Gresham" was a half block to the east. I wasn't old enough to legally watch my sister so our blind roommate, Jude, watched us.

Funny, but not a metaphor.

The apartment had only two bedrooms, but Jude insisted that the walk-in closet was the perfect space for her. She said it was easier for her to know where everything was in a smaller environment. She said she'd rather be in a pond than an ocean.

One day Jude brought her new boyfriend home and he said, "They put you in the closet?"

"She likes it in there," Mom said with all seriousness.

Jude's boyfriend shook his head at the floor and said, "White people."

I remember thinking that was a strange thing to say since Jude, his girlfriend, was white. I wondered if she even knew what "white" meant. How do you describe color to a blind person?

Red is the rage in your gut?

White is the closeting of the disabled?

One day, Jude moved out of our apartment and in with her boyfriend and her room became a closet again.

We saw her a little, and then not at all.

When I got older, I gave my soccer trophies—the plastic, gold figurines eternally almost-kicking their little gold balls—to Goodwill. I got rid of my faux leather briefcase but kept the birthday cards and pictures that were inside.

Then, one year, I spring-cleaned the birthday cards away.

My wife and I began archiving our new family, and my briefcase pictures got mixed in with the rest of them. Our two sons grew. I became an uncle. My grandfather remarried and maybe went crazy, and then maybe not so crazy, and now lives somewhere in-between. That's the way the mind breaks down in our family, in every family that lives long enough.

My mother still has the same smile she had when I was young. She'll probably always have it. My sister still feels everything in big ways and filters it into colors and words. She probably always will.

Right now, I'm typing this in the place where I always write. My computer is in front of me, a bunch of CDs towering on either side, a couple of guitars hanging on the wall, a record player, a thesaurus, an Oxford dictionary.

A copy of a "Feelings Circle" is tacked to my left. It's supposed to help you develop realistic characters. At the middle of the circle are the words *Fear, Anger, Disgust, Sad, Happy,* and *Surprise.* Each isolated in its own piece of the pie, each emotion splintering off into how it is ultimately played out.

If you follow the word *Surprise* diagonally, toward eight o'clock, it leads directly to *Confused,* and from there to either *Perplexed* or *Disillusioned.* The end points of *Anger* fan up and out, leading to sixteen possibilities you could probably already guess at. If you put your finger on *Happy* and ride the line down to six o'clock, between *Accepted* and *Powerful,* you end up on the line that separates *Fulfilled* and *Courageous.*

All of this is printed on a sheet of paper that's four hundred millimeters long by four hundred millimeters wide and one millimeter thick. The entire array of human experience is displayed on what at first appears only to be a cheap imitation of the Mayan calendar.

In about five years, when our youngest son is finished with school, my wife and I plan to move to the coast—north of where my grandfather swam and south of the spot where my sister and I found our piece of foam.

When we move, it will be the first time my wife has ever lived outside of Portland. It's been a long time since I've lived anywhere else.

"Think of all the things that had to happen for us to have even met," she says one night while we're lying in bed.

And I do.

I close my eyes. I squeeze my arm around her. I picture everything that had to happen. I listen to our breath.

In my mind, I put one finger on the word *Happy* at the center of the circle. I make a diagonal line, through the Mayan Calendar of Emotions, to 5:30. My finger passes through *Peaceful.* It lands on the line separating *Hopeful* and *Loving.*

And then the line disappears.

And all that's left is the air we're recirculating, our lungs rising and falling together.

The Process

I don't kill things, and I don't like watching things die.

I don't hunt. I'm not a soldier. I'm not a sadist. But I do lay mice traps. I just now thought of that. I do kill things. I dump their tiny carcasses into plastic bags that are picked up at the corner every other Tuesday. I swat at houseflies with zeal. I don't even use the mouse pelt and meat for clothing or food, I dump the entire body. I don't use the smeared fly blood for crimson paint. I am wasteful.

I've been fishing and liked it.

I eat crab and hamburgers and chicken freed of their heads and feet and mouths and beaks. I consume bacon without exception. I devour veal. I watch war documentaries and support assisted suicide. I don't own a gun, but I sleep with a bat under my bed to pummel possible intruders. It's aluminum.

Sometimes I give money to a beggar. But if those beggars imbibe or freebase and overdose later with my money, am I culpable for their deaths? Does it matter that I give if the giving is part of their destruction? But, I still give. So I must also destroy. And I'm still hungry. Always hungry. Or searching. Or cold. Or sick of something.

I mow lawns with combustible engines. I burn the wood of murdered trees. I take antibiotics for days.

I'd like to think I'd only kill if I had to, but I kill indiscriminately, I kill instinctually. I kill time and semen and plaque unabashedly. I've flushed sea monkeys down toilets—not to expand their vision, but solely to get rid of them—and have undoubtedly contaminated their environment, polluted their minds, orphaned their children. If justice were poetic, those sea monkeys would come back for me after colonizing and establishing better weaponry in the city's sewer systems.

And when they come back, I'll nod, and I'll be expecting them, and I'll say, "I don't kill things, I destroy entire civilizations! I premeditate! What are you going to do about it?!"

I lay 401Ks and Google Map pages and weather forecasts at the graveside of spontaneity. I wash my hands fifteen times a day. I drive cars and slaughter songs and blow out candles in celebration of my existence. I extinguish flame with the best of them. I strangle blind love at reason's wake. I act when action is irrelevant.

I can't save anybody, even if I say, "No one's dying on my watch today!"

And I know, because I've tried saying that, and it doesn't work—not even in the movies.

I drink whiskey and IPA and wonder why some brain cells die while others won't ever leave, why some scenes remain so potent. Why some lovers lie, and other lovers lie badly on beds that they have or haven't made.

I watch things die, and it is not romantic or peaceful or well-acted, but maybe it is natural; maybe it is necessary.

I kill in silent ways, because it's easier to kill in cold blood if the blood is never acknowledged, if the screams have no range, if the smiles have no faces. Even before flat screen TVs and dental plans and personal tragedy and organized faith, we've killed. I've killed.

I kill with or without sharp objects in broad daylight and dark caves. I kill consciousness and set mousetraps and smash flies because I know that whatever I don't kill will eventually come back to kill me.

I take a deep breath, and I kill.

I exhale, and create.

Inhale, kill.

Exhale, create.

I Inhale kill.

I Exhale...

Acknowledgments

This book couldn't have been made without a village.

Much gratitude to...

My beautiful wife, Julie, and amazing sons. My adventurous mom and sister. Every meal, extra bed, and sympathetic ear afforded me by the Morales Family, the Simpson Family, and the Dixon Family. Cats In The Dumpster reading group (Sally, Jess, Jonathan, Fuf, Rockne, Lu, Caitie, Elyssa, Naomi, and Diana) for your fine critique and incredible talent. Post 134 on Alberta Street. Sean Davis. Jude Brewer. Davis Slater. Daniel Krug. Lidia Yuknavitch for helping to invoke the voice of a fellow misfit (I'm forever grateful). Everybody I've ever read with. Everybody who ever answered the 162nd MAX stop payphone in the '90s and yelled out the names of friends we were looking for. Every person I made bad decisions with. Every person I made good decisions with. Everybody inbetween. All the people I've shared an ambulance, engine, or scene with. Everybody who has liked or hated this book, and told other people how much they liked or hated this book. You (for reading every word of the Acknowledgments Page, I thought I was the only one that did that). Black Bomb Books and Jennifer Fulford for giving my made-up words their full attention and building a tangible home for them. And finally, to all my people (every last one of you) you know who you are. Thanx.

About the Author

Jason Arias lives in Portland, Oregon.

To find more of his work visit JasonAriasAuthor.com.

CPSIA information can be obtained
at www.ICGtesting.com
Printed in the USA
FSHW012253070119
54876FS

9 780998 011653